The Age of Dinosaurs in Virginia and Nearby States

THE AGE OF DINOSAURS
IN VIRGINIA AND NEARBY STATES

ROBERT E. WEEMS, PH.D.

BELLE ISLE BOOKS
www.belleislebooks.com

ISBN: 978-1-953021-77-9
LCCN: 2022910945

Printed in the United States of America

Published by
Belle Isle Books (an imprint of Brandylane Publishers, Inc.)
5 S. 1st Street
Richmond, Virginia 23219

BELLE ISLE BOOKS
www.belleislebooks.com

belleislebooks.com | brandylanepublishers.com

ACKNOWLEDGMENTS

The author gratefully acknowledges Jack and Theresa Rayburn, the Maryland Geological Society, Michael Folmer, and Gary Grimsley for their generous donations that greatly helped to cover the cost of publishing this volume. In great measure, it is because of this help that an introduction to *The Age of Dinosaurs in Virginia and Nearby States* is now a reality. Thanks also go to Christina Kann, Haley Simpkiss, and Michael Hardison at Brandylane Publishers, and to Gary Grimsley and Bonnie Weems for their combined help in getting the text both readable and better organized. Without their collective help, this volume would be far less useful than it is now.

Contents

Acknowledgments . . . . *v*

Chapter 1—*The Age of Dinosaurs in Virginia and Nearby States: What We Know and How We Know It* 1

Chapter 2—*Late Triassic, Early Carnian: Triassic Survivors of the Great End-Permian Extinction* 16

Chapter 3—*Late Triassic, Late Carnian: Heyday of the Archosaurs* 26

Chapter 4—*Late Triassic, Norian: Drying Land and Desert Landscapes* 35

Chapter 5—*Late Triassic, Rhaetian: The Curtain Closes on the Triassic World* 45

Chapter 6—*Early Jurassic, Hettangian: The Dawn of the Jurassic World* 49

Chapter 7—*The "Great Hiatus" in the Stratigraphic Record of Eastern North America* 56

Chapter 8—*Early Cretaceous, Early Albian: The Apex of the Age of Dinosaurs in Virginia* 65

Chapter 9—*Late Cretaceous, Cenomanian: The Beginning of Appalachia* 78

Chapter 10—*Late Cretaceous, Campanian: Later Life on the Continent of Appalachia* 85

Chapter 11—*Late Cretaceous, Maastrichtian: The End of the Mesozoic World and the Dawn of the Cenozoic Era* 100

Epilogue—*Where to See Mesozoic Fossils and Exhibits Related to Virginia* 113

References Cited 117

Appendix 1: *Superscript Notes from Text* 137

Appendix 2: *Source Credits for Figures* 153

Table 1: *Vertebrate Fossils Described from the Mesozoic Strata of Virginia and Nearby States* 160

About the Author 177

CHAPTER

1

THE AGE OF DINOSAURS IN VIRGINIA AND NEARBY STATES:
WHAT WE KNOW AND HOW WE KNOW IT

"The Age of Dinosaurs" readily evokes an image of a lost time when large, reptilian creatures roamed the Earth and dominated its landscape for many millions of years. This image is largely correct, except that many of these creatures were probably feathered and more bird-like than reptilian in their appearance and behavior. In recent decades, the *Jurassic Park* and *Jurassic World* films have greatly helped to bring reasonably accurate renditions of many of these creatures to life in the popular mind. But where within the vastness of prehistoric time did each of these creatures live? Which of them lived in Virginia? And how do we know?

The beginning of the Age of Dinosaurs can be defined as the point in the geologic record where the earliest species of ancestral dinosaur appeared, which gave rise to all of the various subsequent descendant branches of the dinosaur family tree (Figure 1). For many decades, the identity of this ancestor remained shrouded in mystery, but in recent years an animal named *Nyasasaurus*, found in Tanzania, has been plausibly proposed to be either the ancestral species of all dinosaurs or an extremely close relative of it.[1] This animal lived about 243 million years ago, which was less than ten million years after the greatest extinction event in Earth's history. "The Great End-Permian Extinction Event" happened 252 million years ago and wiped out about 95% of all marine life and nearly 70% of all terrestrial vertebrate life on our planet.[2] The fact that dinosaurs first appeared about ten million years after this devastating extinction event strongly suggests that the dinosaur dynasty, along with their closest relatives, the pterosaurs, arose and diversified as a direct consequence of the massive global disruptions that the End-Permian Extinction Event caused. This extinction event, by destroying most of the species then living

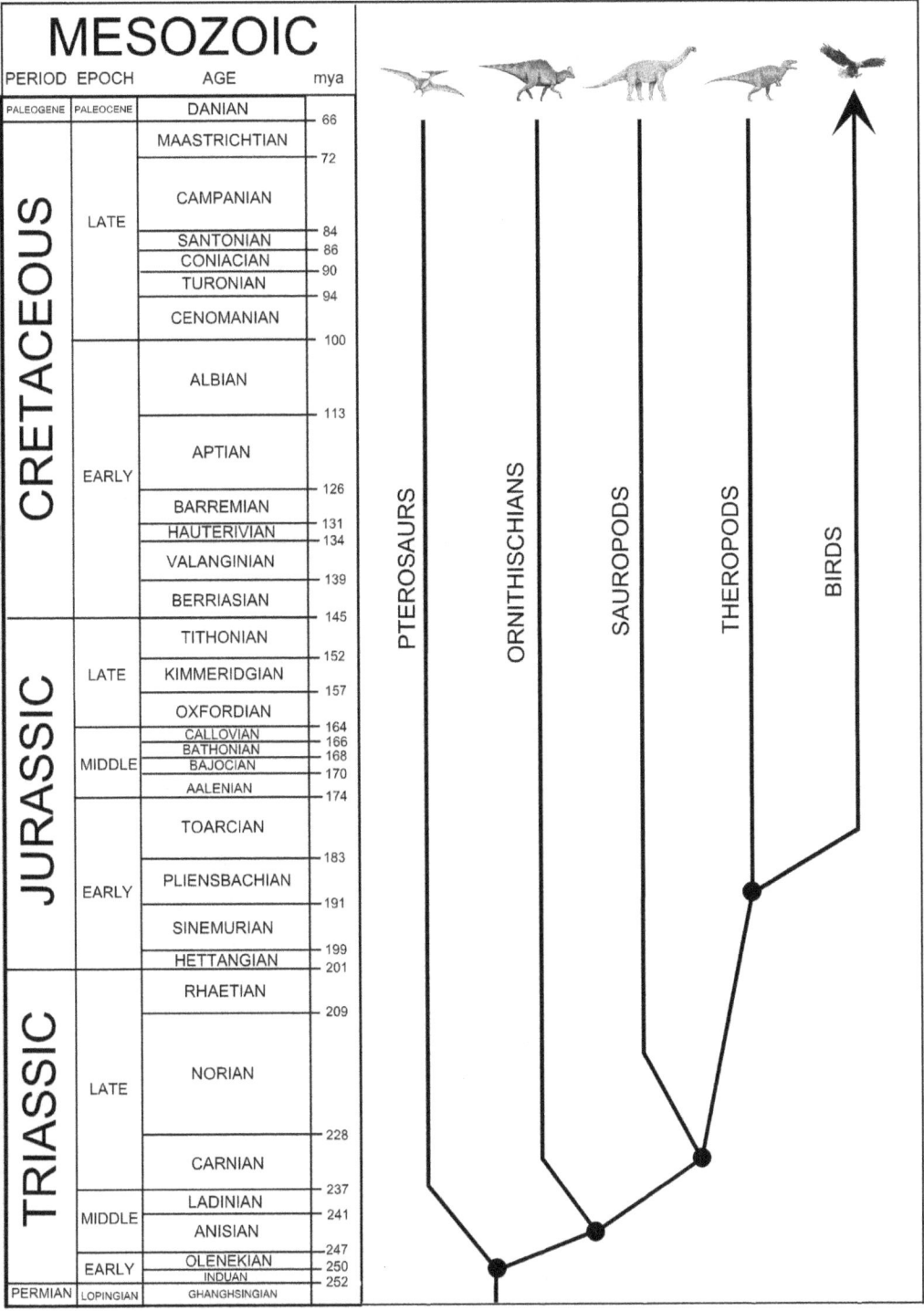

Figure 1 - The Mesozoic time scale and the branches of the dinosaur-pterosaur family tree.

on Earth, opened up vast opportunities for the few survivors of that dreadful catastrophe.

While the discovery of *Nyasasaurus* establishes quite closely the time of origin of the dinosaurs as a group, it does not necessarily establish the beginning of what we might best call the "Age of Dinosaurs." This is because, when dinosaurs first appeared, they were relatively small and unimposing animals that were not especially noticeable in the world in which they lived. For this reason, one easily can argue that the Age of Dinosaurs did not truly begin until about two hundred million years ago, when the dinosaurs indisputably became the "biggest and baddest" animals living in their world. For purposes of this book, however, the early part of dinosaur history is included as a part of the Age of Dinosaurs because a large part of that early record is represented in the rock record of Virginia.

Defining the end of the Age of Dinosaurs has become somewhat complicated in recent decades because many professional students of dinosaurs consider birds to be living dinosaurs. In terms of ancestry this is reasonable enough, for birds are closely related to and descended from a common ancestor within the group of dinosaurs called theropods, which encompass the meat-eating branch of the dinosaur family (Figure 1).[3] Even so, birds constitute only one of four major dinosaur lineages and, at the end of the Mesozoic, even the birds were nearly wiped out by that event. Therefore, it remains most logical to place the end of the Age of Dinosaurs at 66 million years ago, when all dinosaurs and close relatives except for a few birds became extinct in the midst of the world's second greatest global catastrophe.

When defined by these boundaries, the age of dinosaurs lasted from 243 million years ago until 66 million years ago (Figure 1). This age encompassed a time span of almost 180 million years. It is more than a little humbling to realize that the Age of Mammals, in which we now live, has lasted only 66 million years so far, and that is barely more than a third as long as the time during which non-avian dinosaurs roamed and dominated our planet Earth.

❖ ❖ ❖

The science of placing rock strata into their appropriate places within the global geologic time framework is called *stratigraphy*. What we know about the stratigraphy of the Age of Dinosaurs in Virginia is necessarily limited to what we can learn from rock strata that were deposited in Virginia and nearby regions during the Mesozoic Era, which was the time interval within which the non-avian dinosaurs lived and ruled. Unfortunately, the Mesozoic stratigraphic record in Virginia is decidedly spotty (Figure 2). Even so, especially when the Virginia record is combined with the record preserved in nearby North Carolina, Maryland, Delaware, southern Pennsylvania, and southern New Jersey, there is enough information to paint a fairly detailed picture of what was happening in Virginia during that distant age and to tell us much about what kinds of dinosaurs and other animals lived here during the Mesozoic Era.

The rock strata that formed during the Mesozoic Era have been divided globally into three subdivisions called the Triassic Period (252 to 201 million years ago), the Jurassic Period (201 to 145 million years ago), and the Cretaceous Period (145 to 66 million years ago). The strata within each of these periods have been further subdivided into smaller units of time called *epochs*, and each epoch has been subdivided into still smaller units of time called *stages*. Within the Mesozoic Era, epochs are simply designated as Lower, Middle, and Upper for the Triassic and Jurassic, and Lower and Upper for the Cretaceous. Even though the Cretaceous is the longest of the three periods of the Mesozoic, no "Middle Cretaceous" has ever been defined and accepted by the international stratigraphic community. When talking about the rocks that belong to specific stratigraphic units, geologists use the terms "lower," "middle," and "upper" in reference to their relative positions within the global

MESOZOIC

PERIOD	EPOCH	AGE	mya	Land Vertebrate Faunal Stages	SUPER-GROUP	GROUP	FORMATION
PALEOGENE	PALEOCENE	DANIAN	66	Puercan			
CRETACEOUS	LATE	MAASTRICHTIAN	72	Lancian / Edmontian / Kirtlandian	(See Figure 25 for detailed stratigraphy within the Late Cretaceous interval)		
		CAMPANIAN	84	Judithian			
		SANTONIAN	86				
		CONIACIAN	90				
		TURONIAN	94				
		CENOMANIAN	100				
	EARLY	ALBIAN	113		MAR-QUE-SAS	POTOMAC	PATAPSCO / ARUNDEL / PATUXENT
		APTIAN	126				
		BARREMIAN	131	Not Yet Defined			
		HAUTERIVIAN	134				
		VALANGINIAN	139				
		BERRIASIAN	145				
JURASSIC	LATE	TITHONIAN	152				
		KIMMERIDGIAN	157				
		OXFORDIAN	164				
	MIDDLE	CALLOVIAN	166				
		BATHONIAN	168				
		BAJOCIAN	170				
		AALENIAN	174				
	EARLY	TOARCIAN	183				
		PLIENSBACHIAN	191				
		SINEMURIAN	199	Dawan			
		HETTANGIAN	201	Wassonian	NEWARK	MERIDEN	HAMPDEN / EAST BERLIN / HOLYOKE / SHUTTLE MEADOW / TALCOTT
TRIASSIC	LATE	RHAETIAN	209	Apachean			
		NORIAN	228	Revueltian		CHATHAM	PASSAIC
		CARNIAN	237	Adamanian / Otischalkian			LOCKATONG / STOCKTON / DOSWELL
	MIDDLE	LADINIAN	241	Berdyankian			
		ANISIAN	247	Perovkan			
	EARLY	OLENEKIAN	250	Nonesian			
		INDUAN	252	Lootsbergian			
PERMIAN	LOPINGIAN	GHANGHSINGIAN					

Figure 2 – The Mesozoic stratigraphic record preserved in Virginia. Source for figure shown in Appendix 2.

stratigraphic column. When referring to the age of these units, however, the terms "early," "middle," and "late" are used to emphasize their relative time positions within the history of the Earth.

Mesozoic rocks and sediments in Virginia fall within two large stratigraphic packages called *supergroups*. These are subdivided into a hierarchy of smaller packages called *groups*, which are in turn subdivided into even smaller units called *formations* (Figure 2). In some cases, formations have been divided into still smaller subdivisions called *members*. The Late Triassic and Early Jurassic Mesozoic strata in Virginia all belong within the Newark Supergroup. The stratigraphy of this supergroup has been deciphered most successfully through the use of tiny crustaceans called conchostracans, or fairy shrimp.[4] Eggs of modern species of these animals can be raised in aquaria and are sold to children under the name "sea monkeys." These animals' eggs are very resistant to drying, and are tiny and thus can be blown far and wide by the wind. As a group they evolve quite rapidly, so they change quickly by geologic timescale standards. Just as important, they live within tiny bivalved shells that are often buried in the lake-bottom sediments where they live and thus are likely to become preserved as fossils. All of these traits make conchostracans a nearly ideal "index fossil" group for making detailed correlations of nonmarine strata across the early Mesozoic continents of the northern hemisphere, including the strata of the Newark Supergroup. In places where conchostracans have not been found, fossil pollen may be preserved that provides a somewhat less precise but still very useful age determination for the beds in which it occurs.

In Virginia, Mesozoic rocks and sediments younger than the Newark Supergroup belong to the Lower Cretaceous Marquesas Supergroup (Figure 2). Upper Cretaceous rocks, which are not found at the surface in Virginia but are present in nearby states, belong to the Ancora Supergroup, which will be discussed starting in Chapter 9. The coastal to marine environments in which the strata of the Marquesas and Ancora supergroups accumulated were markedly different from the inland, often dry environments in which the Triassic and Jurassic Newark Supergroup strata formed. As a consequence, conchostracans are not very helpful in these younger beds. Instead, in the Cretaceous sequences preserved in Virginia and surrounding states, pollen and microscopic marine fossils are used to help assign these strata to their proper places within the global Mesozoic stratigraphic framework.

The only reason that any record of the early Mesozoic Era exists in Virginia is because that is when the North Atlantic Ocean and Caribbean Sea basins began to form and spread. The origin and development of these features defined both the geography and the environments under which the Mesozoic stratigraphic record in Virginia would accumulate. During the early stages of the birth of the North Atlantic Ocean Basin, fracture lines formed that defined where early Mesozoic strata would become preserved in Virginia (Figure 3). At the beginning of this event during the Triassic Period, Virginia was part of a vast supercontinent named Pangaea that included most of the continental rocks of the modern world (Figure 4). In those days, Virginia was a land-locked, eroding upland whose closest seashores lay far to the west, in what is now the western United States, and to the east in Northern Africa and Western Europe. Back then, the North Atlantic Ocean and the Caribbean Sea did not even exist.

In the Late Triassic, deep forces began to stir within the mantle of the Earth that began to fracture and then pull apart Pangaea. This created rift valleys that began to accumulate sediment, similar to what is happening now in the East African rift valleys and the Rio Grande Rift System in New Mexico and Colorado. This area of rifting in Virginia included the region now called the Piedmont Province and also areas farther east beneath what is now called the Virginia Coastal Plain (Figure 3). Very near the end of the Triassic and continuing into the earliest Jurassic, huge volumes of volcanic magma rose upward through the crust of what is now eastern North America and also parts of western Europe, north-western Africa, and northern South America. In eastern North America, this magma spread across the rift valley lowlands as vast sheets of basaltic lava. By the Middle Jurassic, continued upwelling of basaltic magmas immediately to the east of Virginia (beneath the axis of the newly form-ing mid-Atlantic Ridge) strongly lifted the overlying portions of Pangaea upward and caused profound erosion of this entire uplifted region. Soon after, as seafloor-spreading began in earnest along the nascent mid-At-lantic Ridge, Pangaea began to break apart as the North Atlantic Ocean Basin formed and began to widen. The modern North American tectonic plate, which includes Virginia along its eastern edge, was created by this event, and as this new tectonic plate began to move northwestward, its eastern margin began to sink as it pulled away from the uplifted mid-At-lantic ridge region.

As the eastern coastal region of North America sank below sea level during the Late Jurassic, deposits of sediment began to accumulate across the area that now lies beneath the offshore shallow marine continental shelf of Virginia and other eastern American Seaboard states. Fifty million years later, during the Early Cretaceous, at or near the time when South America began to rift and drift away from Africa, the eastern margin of Virginia sank even further, which caused deposition along its eastern bor-der to spread much farther westward than it had before to approximately the location of modern Interstate Highway 95.[5] This event established the western boundary of what we now call the Virginia Coastal Plain. These events determined that, from the late Jurassic forward, an extensive late Mesozoic stratigraphic record in Virginia and nearby states would be created and preserved only in the Coastal Plain region and its offshore submarine extension beneath the Atlantic continental shelf.

The newly formed North American tectonic plate began to drift mostly westward away from the mid-Atlantic Ridge region where it had been born, but its motion included a persistent northward component

LOCALITIES

15. Potomac-Rappahannock outcrops
14. James-Appomattox outcrops
13. Culpeper Basin
12. Barboursville Basin
11. Scottsville Basin
10. Taylorsville Basin
 9. Deep Run Basin
 8. Flat Branch Basin
 7. Richmond Basin
 6. Farmville Basin
 5. Briery Creek Basin
 4. Roanoke Creek Basin
 3. Randolph Basin
 2. Scottsburg Basin
 1. Danville Basin

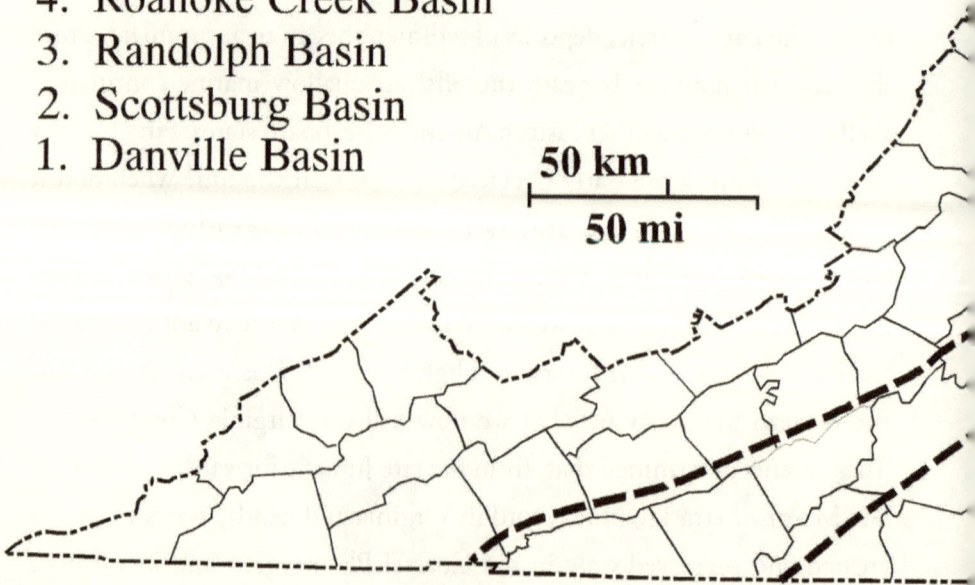

50 km
50 mi

Blue Ridge

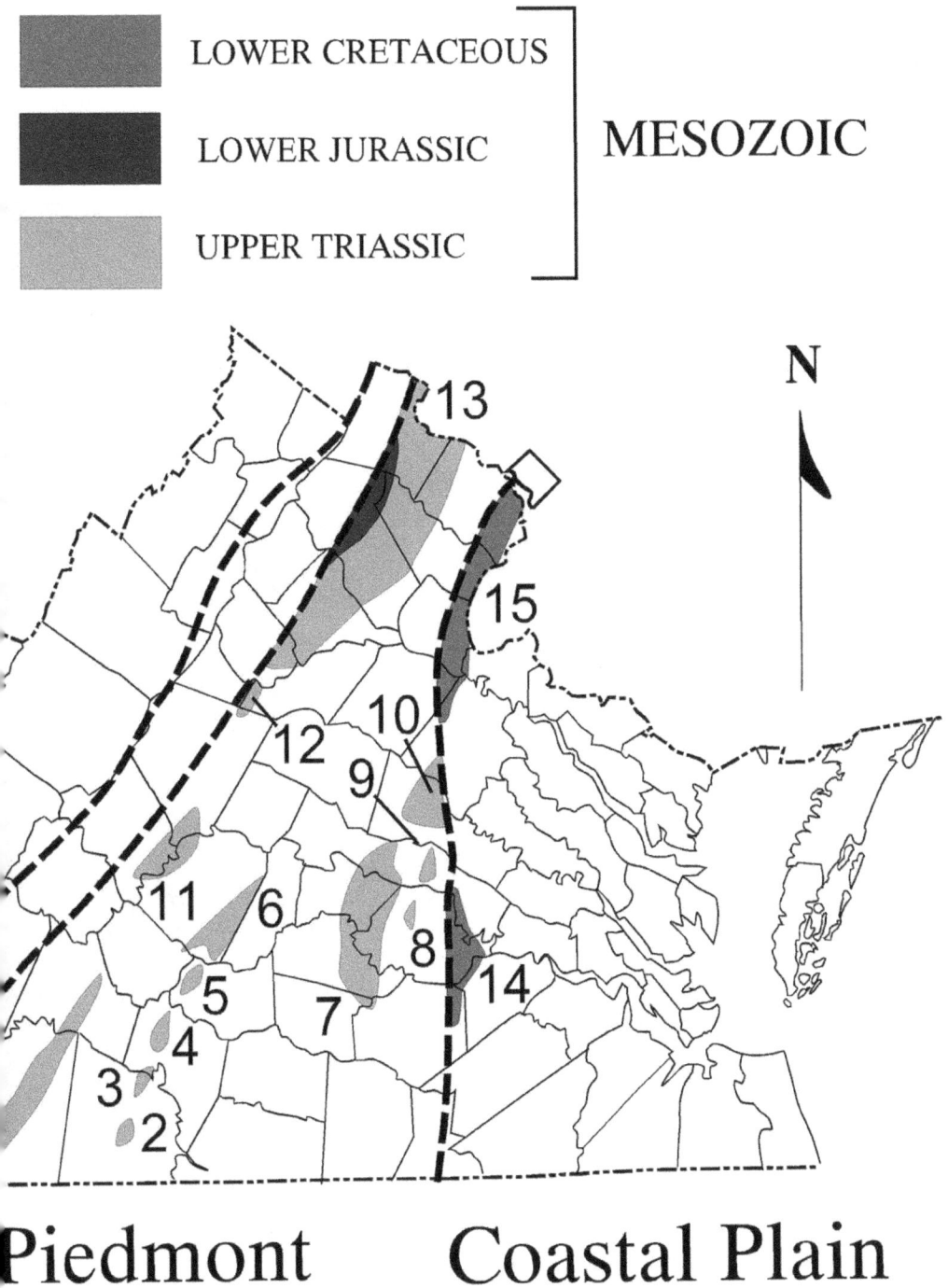

Figure 3 – Places in Virginia where Mesozoic strata are found.
Source for figure shown in Appendix 2.

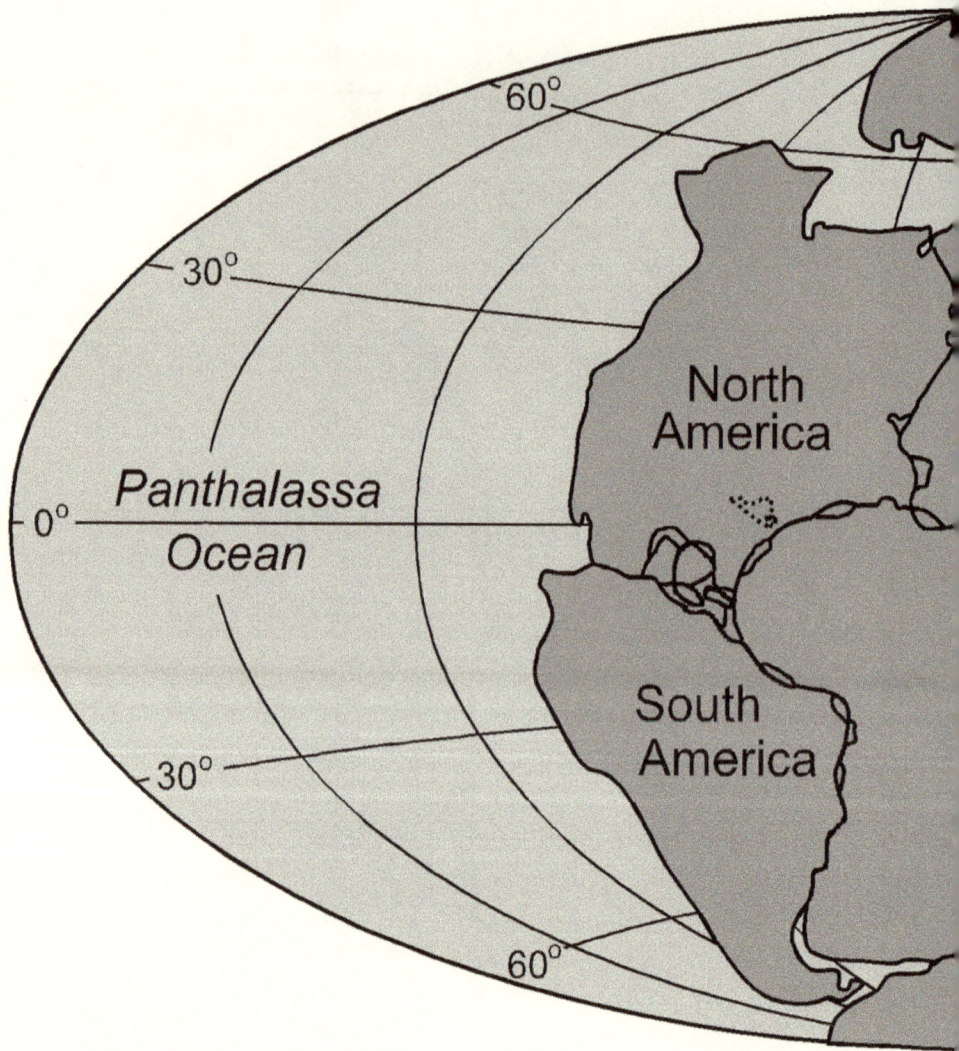

60°

30°

North
America

Panthalassa
Ocean

0°

30°

South
America

60°

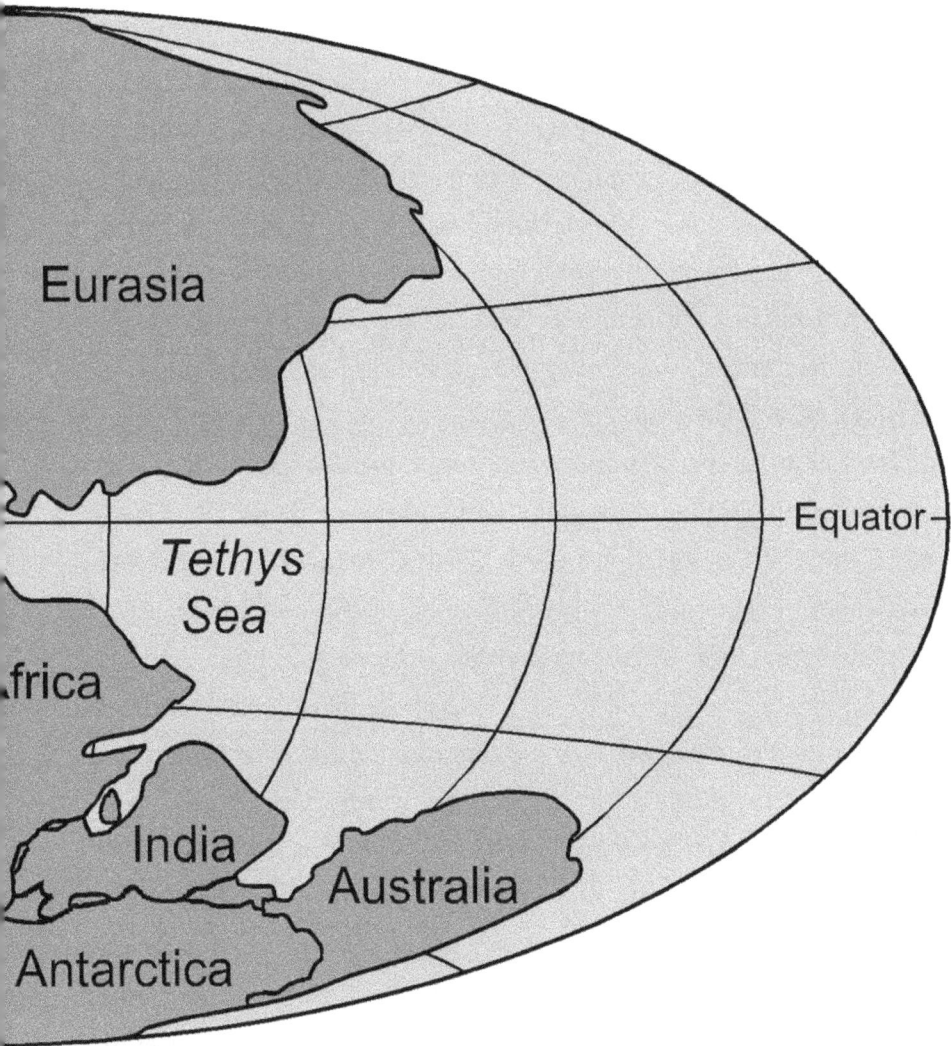

Figure 4 – The location of Virginia within Pangaea (dashed lines) during the early Mesozoic Era. Source for figure shown in Appendix 2.

that has caused the North American continent, including Virginia, to drift slowly but steadily northward as well. In the early part of the Late Triassic, Virginia lay about ten degrees north of the equator within the northern equatorial belt (Figure 4). Since then, the northward component of motion of the North American tectonic plate has resulted in Virginia moving from where it lay early in the Late Triassic into the low latitude desert belt where it lay late in the Late Triassic. By the Cretaceous, Virginia had continued to drift ever farther northward until it lay in the subtropical belt. Today, long after the time of the dinosaurs, Virginia has continued to drift northward and now lies in the so-called "temperate" belt. This long-term northward component of Virginia's tectonic drift from the tropics to the temperate latitudes has been a very significant factor in determining the climate history of Virginia throughout both the Mesozoic and Cenozoic eras.

The following chapters of this book are organized around the strata that formed in Virginia during successive Mesozoic stages. To a lesser degree, the strata preserved in nearby North Carolina, Maryland, Delaware, southern Pennsylvania, and southern New Jersey also are discussed. The global succession of Mesozoic stages is listed in Figures 1 and 2, and the reader is encouraged to refer to these figures to help keep track of the names and the order of the stages discussed here in subsequent chapters. Much more detail about the global stratigraphic picture is also readily available in reader-friendly form on Wikipedia and other websites that discuss and explain the larger global stratigraphic record of the Mesozoic. Similarly, even though many of the scientific names for the animals discussed here will probably be unfamiliar to most readers, most of these animals are discussed on Wikipedia, which provides much additional information for those interested in learning more. Throughout the text, there are numbers for footnotes collected at the end of the book in Appendix 1. These provide additional commentary and/or information to look up that will provide a more detailed record of particular topics discussed here. Similarly, sources for the artwork used in the figures in this book are collected in Appendix 2, and a chronological summary of all the various fossil animals discussed here is provided in Table 1 at the very end of this book.

The Mesozoic stratigraphic record of Virginia carries evidence of four major gaps, called *unconformities* (Figure 2). The first is an unconformity that includes the lower and middle Triassic. The second includes approximately the upper third of the Norian stage and most of the Rhaetian stage of the Late Triassic. The third unconformity is much longer in duration and encompasses most of the Jurassic and the first half of the Early Cretaceous (the Pliensbachian through Barremian stages in Figures 1 and 2). These two unconformities and important events that occurred during those missing periods are discussed in Chapters 5 and 7, respectively. These unconformities are present throughout eastern North America, so they are irremediable facts of life throughout this part of the world. The fourth Late Cretaceous (Cenomanian-Danian) unconformity is treated differently because the nearby states of New Jersey, Delaware, Maryland, and North Carolina contain abundantly fossiliferous strata that give us a very good idea of what life must have also been like in Virginia during the latter part of the Cretaceous. By making use of all these lines of evidence found in the stratigraphic record in Virginia and nearby states, it is possible to piece together a reasonably clear picture of what this land we call Virginia was like during the Mesozoic Era and the Age of Dinosaurs. As research and discoveries continue in the future, more will be discovered that will surely add many new fascinating details concerning this distant age.

CHAPTER

2

LATE TRIASSIC, EARLY CARNIAN:

TRIASSIC SURVIVORS OF THE GREAT END-PERMIAN EXTINCTION

The oldest surviving Mesozoic strata in Virginia began to accumulate during the early Carnian stage of the Triassic Period (Figure 2). All the Triassic and Jurassic strata preserved in Virginia are part of a major stratigraphic sequence called the Newark Supergroup, which is exposed in more or less isolated structural basins from Nova Scotia in Canada to South Carolina in the United States. The regional stratigraphy of the Newark Supergroup has been recently revised and simplified, as shown in Figure 2.[6] The strata within the Newark Supergroup formed during a time when the land that is now Virginia was part of the vast supercontinent called Pangaea (Figure 4). Pangaea existed from near the middle of the Carboniferous Period, about 335 million years ago, until about 175 million years ago, when it finally broke apart near the Early-Middle Jurassic boundary. During the latter part of Pangaea's history, starting in a few regions during the Late Permian and continuing more regionally through the Triassic into the Early Jurassic, the interior of Pangaea began to fracture and break up into an elongate series of rift valleys separated by uplands. As the surrounding uplands eroded, their rocks and soils washed into the newly formed adjacent lowland rift valleys and began to fill them. The infilling of these valleys produced a sequence of strata that provides us with our earliest glimpses of Triassic life in Virginia. The oldest part of these Virginia Triassic strata is named the Doswell Formation.

The Doswell Formation is found in Virginia along the eastern edge of the Piedmont in the Richmond, Flat Branch, Deep Run, and Taylorsville basins, and in the central Piedmont region in the Farmville, Briery Creek, Roanoke Creek, Randolph, and Scottsburg basins (Figure 3). During the time when this oldest Virginia Triassic formation was accumulating, Virginia was located in the northern portion of the equatorial belt. At this latitude, which is where Costa Rica lies today, the climate of Virginia was tropical and wet, and its lowland regions were densely vegetated. So much vegetation became buried in some of these basins that coal beds formed. The most important of these coal deposits are found in the Richmond Basin, which was a major source of coal in the early history of the state before the Appalachian Carboniferous coal fields were accessible to exploitation. A wide variety of fossil plant and animal remains have been found in the swamp, lake, and lowland deposits that are associated with these Triassic coal deposits.

When stratigraphic and paleontological research first began in Virginia in the early 1800s, economic exploitation of coal resources in the Richmond Basin provided the chance to collect abundant plant and occasional vertebrate remains associated with the coal deposits. Some plant fossils also were found in mines that were started in Doswell strata of the Farmville, Briery Creek, and Taylorsville basins, but these mines were far less productive than the mines in the Richmond Basin and never very economically important. The earliest remains that were found in these basins were compared with fossil remains known from Europe to try to determine the age of the Richmond coal beds relative to the standard geologic time scale that was being created in Europe at that time. These discoveries in Virginia were of enough importance that Charles Lyell, one of the early giants of stratigraphy, came here from Europe to learn more about the fossils that were being found in the Richmond Basin coalfields.[7] Initially, there was controversy as to the exact age of the coal beds because half the plant species found here were not found in Europe. This controversy was eventually resolved, however, and the consensus of geologic opinion turned decisively toward a Triassic age.[8] The plant community found in and near the coal beds in the Richmond and other coal-bearing basins was dominated by relatives of the living horsetails and ferns, and by members of an entirely extinct group known as tree-ferns. In better drained environments surrounding the coal swamps, there were plants related to modern cycads and gingkos, plants that belonged to another entirely extinct group called Bennettitales, and abundant conifers, including a very large tree represented by petrified wood called *Araucarioxylon virginianum* (discussed in more detail at the beginning of Chapter 3).

In recent decades, biostratigraphic zonation based on conchostracans (fairy shrimp) has placed the strata of the Doswell Formation specifically within the early part of the Carnian stage of the Triassic.[4] This time interval has also been defined as the Otischalkian Land-Vertebrate Faunachron (Figure 2), named for the distinctive assortment of land vertebrates that are found within age-equivalent early Carnian strata in the southwestern part of the United States.[9] The list of Otischalkian fauna in Virginia so far includes only 16 types of fossil vertebrates (Table 1), but good exposures of the Doswell Formation are not very common, so it is likely that many more kinds of Doswell Formation fossil vertebrates remain to be found in the future.

Of the 16 types of fossil vertebrates known from the Doswell Formation, one is a freshwater shark (*Lissodus* sp.) and four are freshwater bony fishes (Figure 5). Three of the bony fishes are referable to the genera *Dictyopyge, Cionichthys, and Tanaocrossus*.[10] Fragments also have been found of a freshwater lobe-finned fish that was distantly related to the modern "living fossil" marine coelacanth fish *Latimeria*. These fragments may pertain to the genus *Diplurus*, which is known from diagnostic material found in the Virginia region in the following late Carnian stage.[11] No Otischalkian amphibian remains have been identified in Virginia, but the Doswell Formation also occurs in the Newark Basin in Pennsylvania, and there it has yielded remains of a very large predatory amphibian named *Calamops* [12] that was closely related to a better-known genus in the same family named *Trematosaurus* (Figure 7).

Reptile remains are relatively common, including two genera, *Gomphiosauridion* and *Xenodiphiodon*, which belonged to a very primi-

Lissodus sp.

Dictyopyge macrura

Cionichthys meekeri

Tanaocrossus kalliokoskii

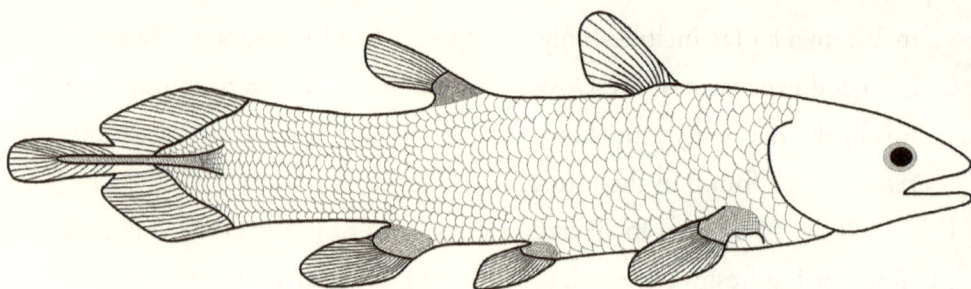

Diplurus longicaudatus

5 cm

Figure 5 – Otischalkian freshwater fishes known from the early Carnian of Virginia. Sources for figure shown in Appendix 2.

tive extinct reptile family known as the procolophonids. These animals, based on their tooth structure, were herbivorous, and their overall appearance was something like that of modern horned toads (see *Leptopleuron* shown in Figure 6) with spikes on their cheeks and short tails.[13] Another lizard-like animal belonged to a group called rhynchocephalians. Rhynchocephalians are represented today by a single genus with two species known as tuataras, which only survive in New Zealand. This group, closely related to modern lizards, was abundant and widespread around the world back in Mesozoic times. The Richmond Basin rhynchocephalian remains are too fragmentary to identify more specifically than to family, but they do show that at least one member of this ancient lizard-like group was in Virginia as far back as the early Carnian.[14]

Two members of this fauna are close to the ancestry of modern mammals.[14] They belonged to a group called therapsids, which first appeared late in the Permian Period prior to the Triassic. Therapsids and their relatives, which collectively were a part of a larger and more diverse group called the synapsids, were the dominant land animals on Earth throughout the Permian Period prior to the appearance of the dinosaurs. Their days of dominance, however, came to an end when the Great End-Permian Extinction Event happened. Most of these animals were exterminated in this catastrophe, but some did survive and, for a while at least, began to increase again in numbers and diversity during the early Triassic Period. Their recovery was only temporary, however, for they were eclipsed near the end of the Carnian by an expanding array of reptiles that largely displaced them except for small, nocturnal members of the group that came to live in environments not favored by the more successful Triassic reptilian groups. During the early Carnian stage, however, the therapsids still were widespread and fairly abundant.

One of these mammal-like reptiles found in the early Carnian in Virginia was an herbivorous animal named *Boreogomphodon jeffersoni*, named for Thomas Jefferson, which belonged to a therapsid group known as the traversodontid cynodonts. It was closely related to *Exaeretodon*, which is shown in Figure 6. The other mammal-like reptile was a rat-sized carnivorous cynodont called *Microconodon*. It was closely related to *Probelesodon*, also shown in Figure 6. A third group of mammal-like animals called dicynodonts also survived into the Triassic. Remains of these animals have been found in the eastern United States in upper Carnian strata, so it is likely that members of this group already were present in the early Carnian and their remains will eventually be found in the lower Carnian Doswell Formation. Neither the dicynodont nor traversodont groups of mammal-like reptiles survived the Triassic, but members of the carnivorous cynodont line did survive and ultimately gave rise to modern mammals, including humans.

Five other kinds of reptiles in this fauna belonged to a group of animals known as archosaurs (Figures 6 and 7), which were the ancestral stock from which crocodiles, pterosaurs, dinosaurs, and birds arose. This group included a rather bizarre long-snouted, armored animal named *Doswellia*, which could fold up much like a modern-day pill bug or horseshoe crab.[15] Also present was *Euscolosuchus* (closely related to *Erpetosuchus* shown in Figure 6) which had spiked armor plates along its back and may have been close to the ancestry of modern crocodiles.[16] A very poorly-known but highly distinctive archosaur named *Uatchitodon* (not pictured) was the earliest animal known to possess teeth with grooves to facilitate the injection of venom into its prey.[14] Two other archosaurs are present in this fauna that can only be identified to their family level. One, known from teeth, represents an aquatic crocodile-like member of the family Phytosauridae.[15] Although these teeth are not truly identifiable below the family level, the only age-equivalent Otischalkian phytosaurs known from the American southwest are *Angistorhynchus* and *Parasuchus*. These teeth likely pertain to one of those two genera. The fifth archosaur, *Poposaurus*, so far known from only two vertebrae and a humerus, was a member of the terrestrial predator family Poposauridae.[15] This animal actually was a crocodilian, but remarkably it had evolved into a predator similar to what the thecodont dinosaurs later would become. These types of archosaurs, or better-known species that are closely related to them, are shown in Figure 7.

The complexion of the Doswell Formation vertebrate fauna is very similar to other vertebrate faunas found in Pangaea during the earlier parts of the Triassic. This rather motley assortment of Triassic survivors of the Great End-Permian Extinction Event were all doing their best to recover, adapt, and diversify into an unfamiliar new world that had opened up around them. At this early point in the Mesozoic Era, it was not at all obvious which of these various contenders would eventually become the big winners in the new and rapidly evolving world. The early Carnian saw a continued prevalence of the mammal-like reptiles, which had dominated the terrestrial world in the Permian Period prior to the Triassic. By the late Carnian, however, things quickly began to change as the mammal-like reptiles' populations rapidly declined and were eclipsed by lizard-like reptiles and archosaur reptiles, which were both part of the ancestral group that gave rise to the later Mesozoic marine reptiles, crocodilians, pterosaurs, and dinosaurs.

Although no evidence of dinosaurs has been found so far in the Doswell Formation, age-equivalent early Carnian strata in Britain and France contain small, very dinosaur-like footprints. These track types also are found in underlying rocks in those same areas that formed during the immediately preceding Ladinian stage (Figures 1 and 2). These footprints tell us that dinosaurs, or their very close bipedal relatives, were wandering about in better-drained environments elsewhere in the world away from the coal swamps of eastern Virginia. The upright, two-legged stance typical of even the earliest dinosaurs was far better suited for scampering about in open upland environments than it was for getting around in the lush, swampy, tropical environments that dominated the swamplands and lake environments in which the Doswell Formation animals lived. The animals found in the Doswell Formation instead were adapted to wet, lowland environments not especially favorable for early dinosaurs. If fossils or footprints are eventually found in the sandy and less swampy riverine and overbank strata that occur in some parts of the Doswell Formation, these may yet provide direct evidence of dinosaurs in Virginia during the early Carnian.

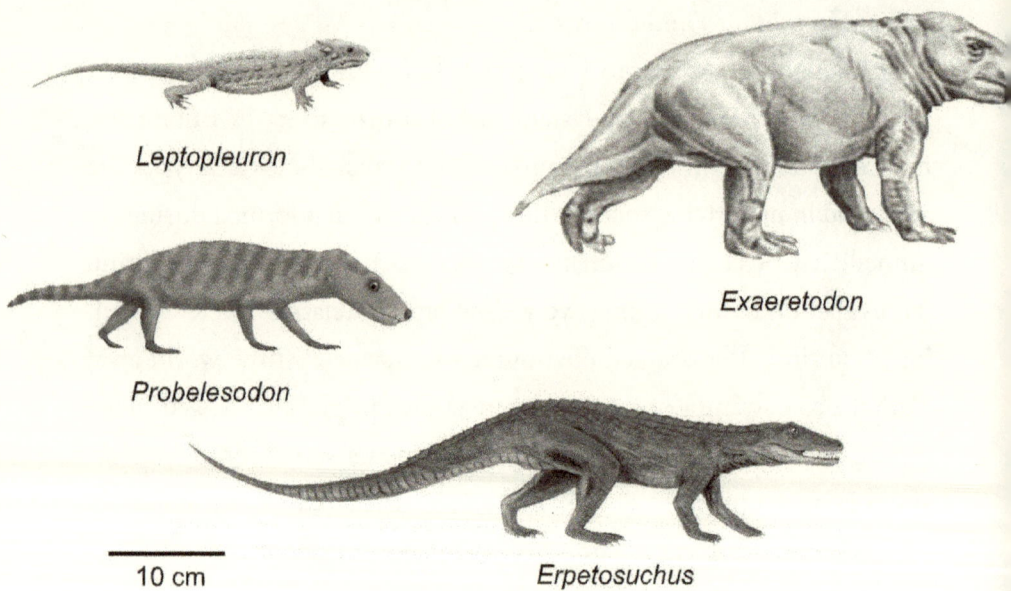

Figure 6 – Smaller land vertebrates closely related to Otischalkian animals from the early Carnian Doswell Formation. Sources for figure shown in Appendix 2.

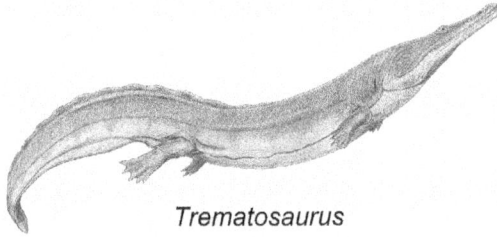

Trematosaurus

Parasuchus

50 cm

Doswellia

Poposaurus

Figure 7 – Otischalkian amphibian and three archosaurs similar or identical to ones found in Virginia. Sources for figure shown in Appendix 2.

CHAPTER

3

LATE TRIASSIC, LATE CARNIAN:

HEYDAY OF THE ARCHOSAURS

During late Carnian time, the Stockton and Lockatong formations were deposited in Virginia and nearby states (Figure 2). The Stockton Formation is widespread, being found in the eastern Piedmont Richmond and Taylorsville basins, the central Piedmont Farmville and Scottsburg basins, and in the western Piedmont Danville/Dan River Basin (Figure 3). The Lockatong Formation is less widespread, being found only in the western Piedmont Dan River/Danville Basin and in the northern part of the Taylorsville Basin, where it is deeply buried beneath the Virginia Coastal Plain. The late Carnian age of the Stockton and Lockatong formations has been established both by conchostracan biostratigraphy[4] and by the fact that the vertebrate fauna discovered within this interval belongs to the age-equivalent late Carnian Adamanian Land-Vertebrate Faunachron (Figure 2).[9]

No animal fossils have been recovered from the Stockton Formation in Virginia, though they are found elsewhere. Even so, in Virginia this formation is notable for the abundant petrified wood, named *Araucarioxylon virginianum*, that has been found within it. This tree is closely related to *Araucarioxylon arizonicum*, preserved as logs in Petrified Forest National Park in Arizona. This was a tree that probably attained a height of about 160 feet (fifty meters) and was rather different in appearance from any living conifer trees.[17] Unlike in Virginia, the Stockton Formation in North Carolina has yielded a number of fossil vertebrate remains in the Durham and Sanford basins in the eastern North Carolina Piedmont.[18]

The Lockatong lake strata in the Danville/Dan River Basin have yielded an exceptional insect fauna that is perhaps the best record of Triassic insects known from anywhere in the world.[19] This formation, both in Virginia and in North Carolina, also has yielded important vertebrate finds. As with the Stockton Formation, many of the best recent discoveries from the Lockatong Formation have been made in its Cumnock Member that is found in the Sanford and Durham basins in the eastern Piedmont of North Carolina.

Globally, the beginning of the late Carnian was an exceptionally wet interval.[20] It was at this time that the Stockton Formation was deposited and large *Araucarioxylon* trees were abundant throughout North America. After Stockton time, however, the climate in most of eastern North America became drier while the Lockatong Formation was being deposited. In the Newark Supergroup basins, this drying event was strongly influenced by an increasing rate of uplift along the fault lines that bordered these basins. In the basins bordered on their western sides by fault scarps, lakes persisted in the valley bottoms, but the climate began to oscillate between wet and dry seasonally. During the dry seasons, alkaline minerals formed that began to accumulate in the lakes. In contrast, a few basins in North Carolina were bordered on their eastern margin by a fault scarp rather than on their western margin. This geometry captured rain from the prevailing winds and allowed humid coal-forming conditions to persist in those basins long after the more regionally humid early Carnian environments had ceased to exist in Virginia.[21]

This regional pattern of valley bottom climates indicates that the prevailing winds in those days blew from the west or northwest. This wind pattern created a "rain-shadow" effect in those basins bounded on their west side by faults and uplifted mountains. As the prevailing winds rose over the western sides of mountains bordering the western sides of these basins, they lost moisture in the form of rain, which then drained westward, away from the valley floors that lay to the east. By the time these winds passed over the mountains, they had limited moisture left to spread across the valley floors lying within the rain shadows of these mountains.

In complete contrast, there was increased rainfall in the Durham-Chatham-Sanford string of basins in the eastern Piedmont of North Carolina because those basins were bounded by faults and uplifted mountains on their eastern sides. There, when these basins' eastern margin mountains caused the winds to rise and rain upon their western sides, the resulting rainfall on their western slopes then drained back to the west directly into their adjacent basins, which kept their valleys much wetter than any of the other Newark Supergroup basins at that time.

The late Carnian fish faunas that have been found in the Newark Supergroup basins are very similar to the Triassic freshwater fishes known from strata of the same age in the southwestern United States, but they are different from fossil fish known from age-equivalent strata found elsewhere in the world. This indicates that the river systems that drained the Newark Supergroup basins in the late Carnian drained westward toward the southwestern United States across the central United States.[22] This westward flowing river network, which provided a highway for fish migration, was strikingly different from the river network that exists today, in which the Mississippi River system carries water and sediment from the entire mid-American region between the Appalachians and the Rockies southward into the Gulf of Mexico.

When the late Carnian animals found in Virginia and North Carolina are combined, thirty-one kinds of nonmarine vertebrates are known. This represents a far more diverse fauna than has been found in any other time interval of the Newark Supergroup. It is not yet clear whether the late Carnian was a time of unusually favorable environmental conditions that were able to support an exceptionally diverse array of animals, whether the abundance of collected specimens reflects some sort of a bias in the collecting that has been done, or perhaps a combination of both.

The fossil vertebrates from this interval include a variety of fishes. Four different types of freshwater bony fishes are present (Figure 8) that belong to the genera *Cionichthys*, *Semionotus*, *Synorichthys*, and *Turseodus*. There also were three kinds of lobe-finned fish present that belong

Synorichthys stewarti

Cionichthys meekeri

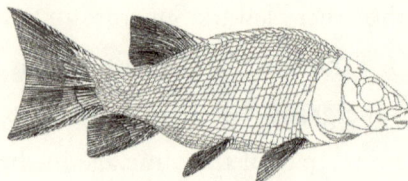

Semionotus sp.

Turseodus acutus

Diplurus newarki

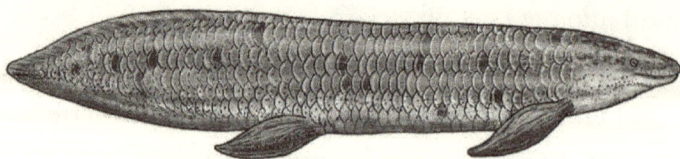

Arganodus sp.

5 cm

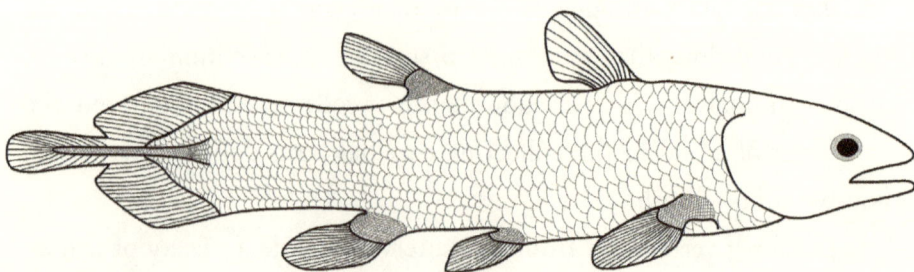

Diplurus longicaudatus

Figure 8 – *Adamanian freshwater fishes known from the late Carnian of Virginia and North Carolina. Sources for figure shown in Appendix 2.*

to the genera *Pariostegus* and *Diplurus*.[23] Teeth of a lungfish (*Arganodus*) also have been reported.[24] A single kind of amphibian, *Dictyocephalus*, is known from these late Carnian deposits. *Dictyocephalus* belonged to a prehistoric family called the Metoposauridae.[25] This animal was closely related to the better known western American species *Koskinonodon* (Figure 9), which was a large ambush predator that lived in the late Carnian lakes and rivers of that time. Among lizard-like reptiles, the presence of the procolophonid reptile *Colognathus* shows that this group persisted from the early Carnian. A taxonomically indeterminate sphenodontid, a relative of the modern tuatara, was also present.[24]

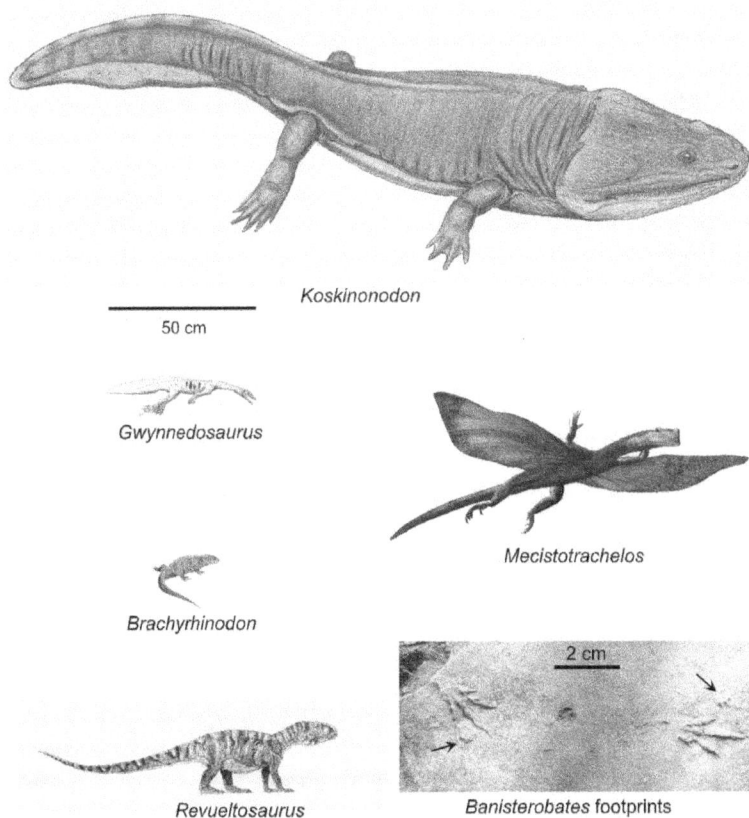

Figure 9 – Typical Adamanian animals known from the late Carnian of Virginia and North Carolina. Sources for figure shown in Appendix 2.

Archosaurian reptiles were more abundant and diverse than they had been in the early Carnian when the Doswell Formation was being deposited. By the late Carnian, this group had come to include 14 distinctly different types. Poorly known but taxonomically distinctive species belong to the genera *Crosbysaurus, Galtonia, Revueltosaurus,* and the earliest known venomous animal, *Uatchitodon.*[24] Better known are *Mecistotrachelos,* which was an early example of a gliding reptile,[26] and *Tanytrachelos*[27] (perhaps synonymous with *Gwyneddosaurus* from the Lockatong Formation of Pennsylvania[28]), which was a long-necked amphibious reptile that inhabited lakes and probably low energy rivers. This animal was an early freshwater example of a group of reptiles that would, later in the Triassic, move into the seas and give rise to a group called the plesiosaurs. Two other members of the archosaur reptile group were large

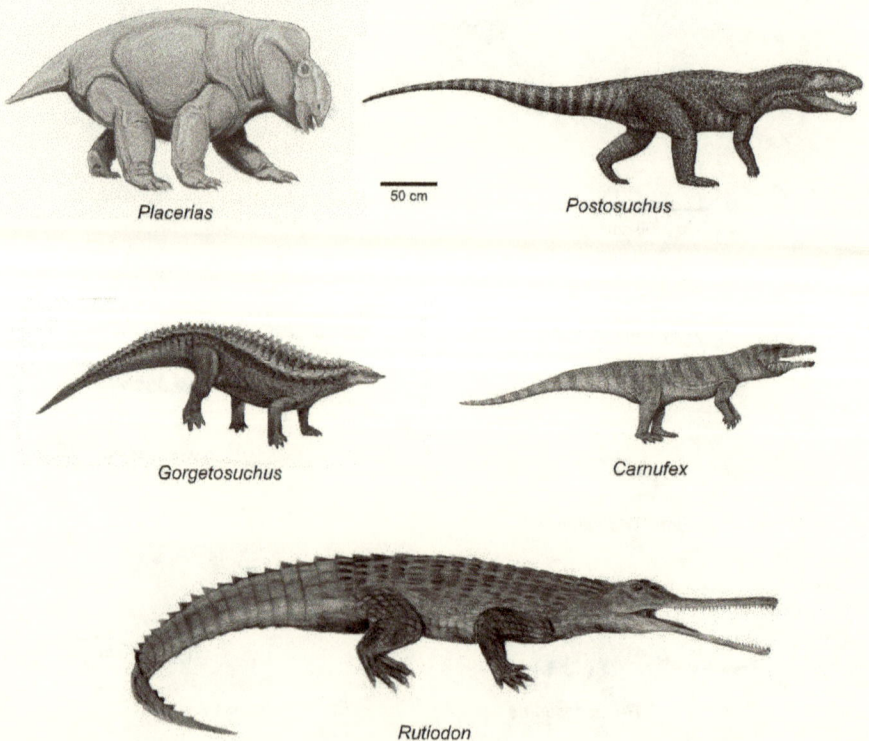

Placerias   50 cm   Postosuchus

Gorgetosuchus   Carnufex

Rutiodon

Figure 10 – *Adamanian archosaurs and a dicynodont known from the late Carnian of North Carolina. Sources for figure shown in Appendix 2.*

rauisuchid carnivores called *Postosuchus*[29] and *Zatomus*,[30] which were probably the top predators in the terrestrial realm at that time (Figure 10). In the aquatic realm, the archosaurian phytosaur *Rutiodon* was the top predator.[31]

By the late Carnian, a family of archosaurs known as aetosaurs had also appeared, and they became specialized for eating vegetation. They had already diversified into three distinct genera (*Coahomasuchus, Lucasuchus,* and *Gorgetosuchus*) that left remains in the North Carolina basins. [32] Finally, two other species of archosaurs were present that were close to the ancestry of crocodilians, *Carnufex*[33] and *Dromicosuchus*.[34] In Virginia and North Carolina, during the late Carnian, the earliest evidence for dinosaurs has been found based on footprints.[35] These footprints have been referred to several footprint genera (called ichnogenera, meaning "trace fossil genera," to distinguish them from biological genera). These are named *Banisterobates, Atreipus,* and *Grallator.* They indicate that, by the late Carnian, at least three kinds of primitive dinosaurs were roaming this region.

The late Carnian Adamanian land vertebrate fauna mostly represents a continuation and diversification of the preceding Otischalkian fauna. Notably missing in the Adamanian fauna are the armored reptile *Doswellia,* the amphibian *Calamops,* and the fish *Dictyopyge,* but many other species had appeared to take their places. Animals that were related to mammals included the two early Carnian cynodont mammal-like reptiles *Boreogomphodon*[36] and *Microconodon*[37], which continued to exist as a minor component of the fauna. Additionally present was a *Placerias*-like dicynodont,[38] which represents the largest herbivore known from the Adamanian fauna of the eastern United States (Figure 10). Most of the new forms that appeared in the Late Carnian were archosaurs, and this shows that archosaurs were becoming a relatively much larger component of the fauna than they had been in early Carnian Otischalkian time. The appearance in this fauna of three new kinds of herbivorous archosaurs belonging to a group called aetosaurs shows that archosaurs were not only becoming more diverse in the habitats they had previously occupied, but that they were also beginning to move strongly into the domain of herbivores, where they previously had not been players. Their proliferation into the grazing habitat probably played a major role in why *Placerias* and similar dicynodonts became rare after late Carnian Adamanian time. Although dinosaurs were not yet a prominent part of the Adamanian faunal realm, they had clearly diversified into a number of distinctly different types, which were becoming much more noticeable within the Adamanian landscape than they had been before.

CHAPTER

4

LATE TRIASSIC, NORIAN:
DRYING LAND AND DESERT LANDSCAPES

The Norian stage of the Triassic was when the Passaic Formation was deposited in Newark Supergroup rift valleys, including five of the basins found in Virginia. Passaic strata are preserved in the eastern Piedmont region only in the northern part of the Taylorsville Basin; these strata are deeply buried beneath the Virginia Coastal Plain. In the western Piedmont, Passaic strata are exposed in the Dan River/Danville Basin, the Scottsville Basin, the Barboursville Basin, and the Culpeper Basin. In most of these basins, the Passaic has yielded few or no vertebrate fossils. The major exception to this is the Culpeper Basin, where significant fossil discoveries have been made that give us our best available picture of what life was like in Virginia during the early and middle parts of the Norian. The Norian age of the Passaic Formation has been established by conchostracan biozones,[4] and this tells us that most of the vertebrate fauna found in the Virginia Passaic Formation belongs to the Revueltian Land-Vertebrate Faunachron.[9] The conchostracan zonation documents that the highest portions of the Passaic should belong within the succeeding Apachean Land-Vertebrate Faunachron, but only a few footprints have been recovered from this upper interval, and these footprints only represent long-ranging ichnotaxa. Thus, there are no vertebrate skeletal remains that can serve to independently verify that the upper part of the Passaic stratigraphic column belongs to the Apachean Land-Vertebrate Faunachron.

Throughout the Norian stage of the Upper Triassic, the Virginia region continued its northward drift into and through the northern latitude desert belt where the Sahara Desert lies today. As Virginia drifted into this belt, the regional climate steadily became more arid as the Norian progressed. In the Culpeper Basin in Virginia, the lowest and oldest part of the Passaic Formation is a unit called the Manassas Sandstone

Member. This unit is composed mostly of relatively well-sorted sand grains that indicate the persistence of a through-flowing river drainage system that flushed finer silt and clay sediments out of the Culpeper Basin downstream toward the western United States, as had been true during Carnian time.[39] As more time passed, however, water flow decreased so much that the immediately overlying unit, the Balls Bluff Siltstone Member, consisted of much finer sediments, which formed in the localized sluggish stream environments that had come to dominate the basin floor during that time.

Above the Balls Bluff Siltstone, the upper two-thirds of the Passaic Formation in Virginia consists of strata that accumulated in playa valley environments, which had shallow alkaline to saline lakes that periodically dried up to form desert floors. The Great Salt Lake valley represents a somewhat similar modern environmental setting. The Culpeper Basin valley floor was flanked on its west by alluvial fans draping down into the Culpeper Basin off of the border fault that bounded the basin on its western side. During most of this time interval, the sediments accumulating on the valley floor consisted of rooted and mud-cracked soils that were full of carbonate minerals. Soils of this type, called "pedocals," accumulate in places where the climate is very dry and, because of this aridity, evaporation exceeds precipitation. Periodically, however, over a cycle that lasted about one hundred thousand years, the climate became wetter for a while, and playa lakes formed to cover most or all of the basin floor. [40] Mudflats would form along the margins of these playa lakes as the water level fluctuated up and down, and animals walking along the lake margins often made footprints that became preserved as the mudflats dried out. These footprints belonged either to animals that lived in the lake and occasionally ventured out of its waters onto land, or to animals visiting the lake margin from more upland areas, probably looking for water, food, or both.

The Revueltian vertebrate fauna found in the lower Passaic Formation in the Culpeper Basin is much less diverse than the fauna recovered from the preceding Adamanian stage. This is probably due in part to the harsher climate that existed in Virginia during this time interval, but it is also at least partly due to the rather limited occurrence of fossiliferous beds of this age in the Culpeper Basin. As the drainage system within the Culpeper Basin became increasingly localized or disappeared altogether, habitats suitable for the survival of fish became limited. Most occurrences of fossil fish in the Passaic Formation in the Culpeper Basin are in the basal Manassas Sandstone Member, because that unit formed before extremely dry conditions came to prevail. Three kinds of bony fish were present (Figure 11), referable to the genera *Cionichthys, Semionotus,* and *Tanaocrossus.* One kind of lobe-finned coelacanth fish, *Diplurus,* has also been found. In the higher members of the Passaic Formation, only scattered fish scales referable to *Semionotus* have been identified, and these are found only in a few of the more fossiliferous playa-lake deposits.[41]

Bones of Triassic reptiles are rarely found in the Culpeper Basin, except for a few phytosaur bones that probably pertain to *Redondasaurus* based on the Revueltian age of their occurrence.[41] Phytosaur tracks, called *Apatopus,* are locally abundant and were likely made by *Redondasaurus.* Other reptiles in this fauna are known only from their footprints (Figure 12). These include footprints called *Rhynchosauroides,* probably made by a lizard-like sphenodontid reptile; *Gwyneddichnium,* probably made by the long-necked aquatic archosaur *Tanytrachelos* that persisted into the Norian from the late Carnian; *Chirotherium,* a small predatory rauisuchid archosaur; and *Brachychirotherium,* a medium-sized herbivorous aetosaur track that was likely made by *Typothorax.* In the subsurface part of the Taylorsville Basin, an aetosaur armor plate was found within a core.[42] Its small size and relatively simple surface texture identify it as belonging to *Aetosaurus,* which is known from far more complete Revueltian-age remains found in New Jersey and Connecticut. It was too small an animal to have made the *Brachychirotherium* footprints found in

A

Tanaocrossus kalliokoskii

B

Cionichthys dunklei

C

Semionotus sp.

2 cm

D

Diplurus newarki

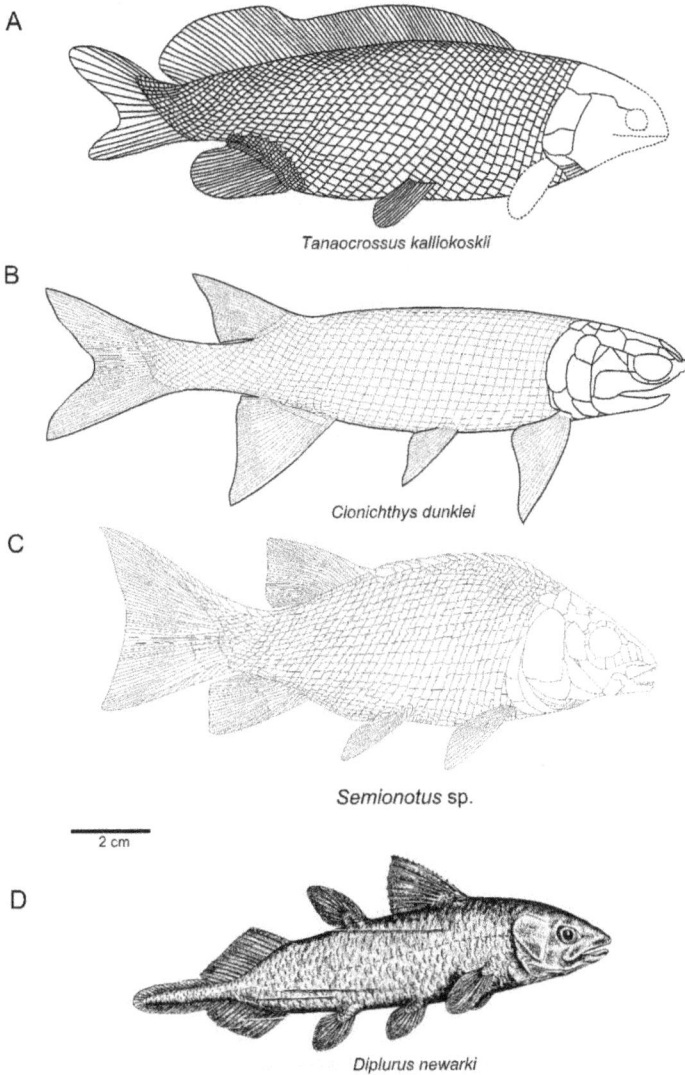

Figure 11 – Typical Revueltian fishes known from the Norian of Virginia. Sources for figure shown in Appendix 2.

the Culpeper Basin, so this indicates that at least two kinds of aetosaurs must have existed in Virginia during the Norian stage of the Triassic.

Unlike in the older Newark Supergroup strata, which were deposited in earlier Otischalkian and Adamanian times, most younger Newark Supergroup footprint-bearing strata in the Culpeper Basin are dominated

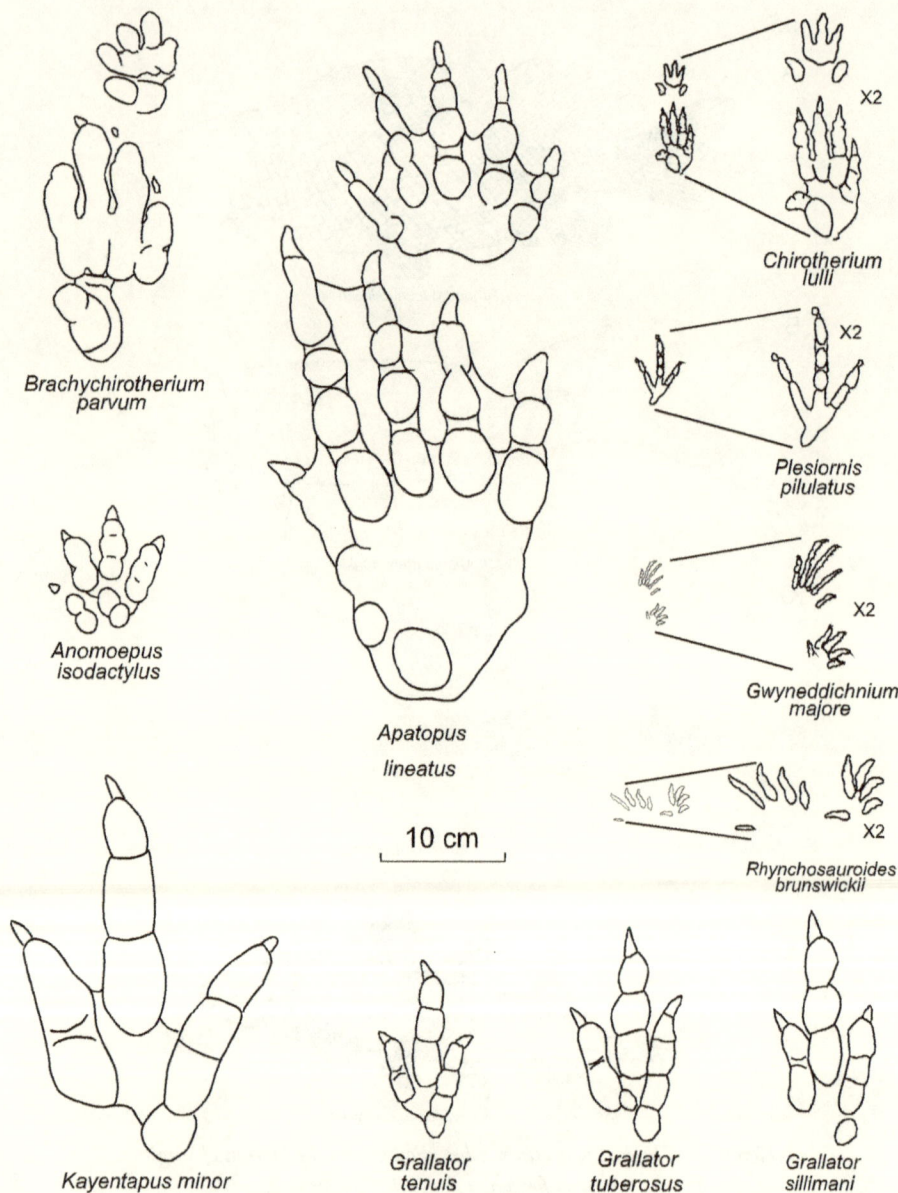

Brachychirotherium
parvum

Anomoepus
isodactylus

Apatopus

lineatus

10 cm

Chirotherium
lulli

Plesiornis
pilulatus

Gwyneddichnium
majore

Rhynchosauroides
brunswickii

Kayentapus minor

Grallator
tenuis

Grallator
tuberosus

Grallator
sillimani

*Figure 12 – Typical Revueltian footprints known from the Norian of Virginia.
Source for figure shown in Appendix 2.*

by dinosaur tracks. These indicate that by Revueltian time, dinosaurs had become quite abundant and diverse in the Culpeper Basin.[41] Footprints representing three distinctly different species of small carnivorous dinosaurs are found, all referable to the ichnogenus *Grallator*. These tracks attest to the presence of a variety of small, agile dinosaurs in this fauna. Some of these footprints, referred to the ichnospecies *G. sillimani*, are very close in size and in their proportions to the feet of the Norian dinosaur *Coelophysis*, best known from numerous skeletons found at Ghost Ranch and nearby areas in New Mexico (Figure 13). A much larger dinosaur, probably the apex predator in this fauna, is represented by tracks called *Kayentapus*. This animal made footprints that were very similar in size and proportions to the feet of *Liliensternus*, which also lived in Norian time and is known from skeletal remains found in Germany. *Plesiornis pilulatus*, a small track that has bird-like proportions, occurs in the lower part of the Virginia Passaic. It is far from certain, however, whether this track type was made by an ancestral bird or by some other type of bird-sized dinosaur long extinct. In either case, what this type of footprint does show is that, even by Norian time, small dinosaurs or dinosaurian bird ancestors were already moving into the small active animal niche that birds would later come to dominate.

Besides these various tracks of theropod dinosaurs, other small dinosaur tracks referable to the ichnogenus *Anomoepus* show the presence of some kind of small, primitive, herbivorous, bipedal ornithischian dinosaur that ran in what could be called herds or flocks. A group of *Anomoepus* tracks found in the Culpeper Quarry showed that larger animals were traveling along the outer edges of this group and smaller animals were traveling toward the middle of the group. This is the best documented evidence for herding in ornithischian dinosaurs as early as the Late Triassic.

In the Gettysburg Basin of southeastern Pennsylvania, a number of tracks have been found in rocks about the same age as the Manassas Sandstone Member in the Culpeper Basin. One of these track types belongs to the ichnogenus *Pentasauropus*, which was made by a large, stubby-toed, quadrupedal animal. It seems likely that the maker of this kind of track was a large dicynodont similar to *Placerias* (Figure 10), though the Pennsylvania tracks are younger than any skeletal remains that have been found of that particular dicynodont genus. However, a very large dicynodont (*Lisowicia*) has been described from the late Norian of Poland (Figure 13), so this group of animals is known to have persisted nearly to the end of the Triassic elsewhere in the world and therefore certainly could have been still present in the early Norian Revueltian fauna of the Virginia region.[43]

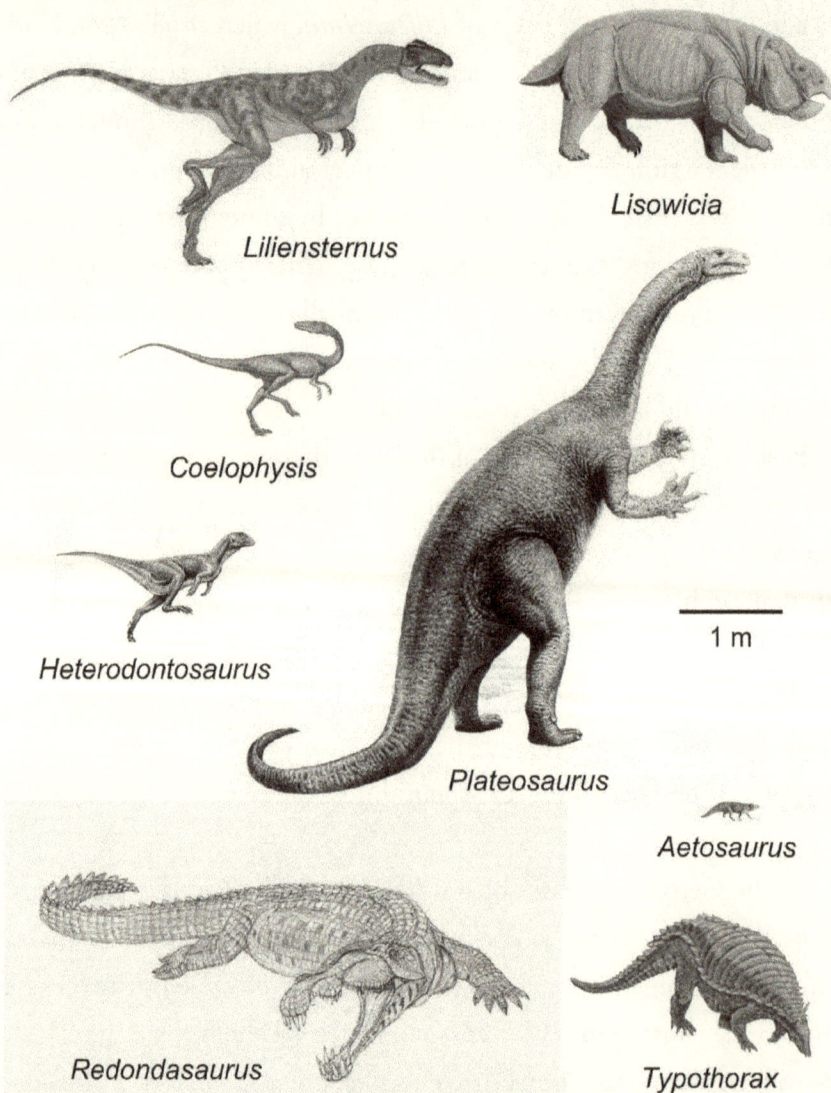

Figure 13 – Possible trackmakers of Norian footprints and a close relative to the gastrolith producer. Sources for figure shown in Appendix 2.

A rather more unusual example of dinosaur remains in the Culpeper Basin is provided by dark reddish-brown, polished, variably rounded pebbles and small cobbles of quartzite and quartz. These gastroliths (literally "stomach-stones") were rounded and polished in the digestive mills of prosauropod dinosaurs. Prosauropods had teeth designed for plucking, which meant that they probably nipped nutritious fruit-like bodies or seeds off of trees and large bushes and swallowed them whole. These fruit-like bodies or seeds would have fallen on the ground in great numbers when they were ripe, at which time many could have been gathered up from the ground and swallowed by prosauropods. Prosauropod teeth were not designed for chewing food, so prosauropods easily could have inadvertently swallowed pebbles and cobbles among the seeds and fruit that were in the same size range as their sought-after food. This is probably why these animals swallowed food-sized rocks that rolled around in their digestive tracks until they became highly polished. Interestingly, these gastroliths have only been found in the rooted and mud-cracked soil beds that lie between the playa lake bed intervals. This indicates that these prosauropod dinosaurs avoided the Norian lake margin environments in the Culpeper Basin, probably because of the presence there of very large phytosaurs that would have been easily capable of killing and eating them.[41]

The Revueltian fauna in Virginia is strikingly different from the Otischalkian and Adamanian faunas that preceded it. The amphibians and all but one kind of mammal-like reptile were gone, as well as most of the archosaurs except for phytosaurs, aetosaurs, and one small rauisuchid. These animals were all replaced by a diversity of dinosaurs that included members of all three of the major extinct dinosaur lineages: carnivorous theropods of both small and large size, large herbivorous prosauropods, and much smaller bipedal herbivorous ornithischians. The abruptness of this faunal transition is not seen in many other parts of the Norian world. In places that were then outside of the low northern latitude desert belt—such as the Germanic Basin in central Europe, where rivers and lakes existed in abundance—amphibians, aquatic archosaurs and mammal-like reptiles persisted and still thrived almost until the end of the Triassic. Turtle remains also began to appear widely across much of the globe, but not here.[44] In Virginia, where Norian strata document the driest and most desert-like environments preserved in our Mesozoic stratigraphic record, these wetter environments and their inhabitants had ceased to exist in the lowland areas where sediment was accumulating. All that remains in Virginia of the Norian world are traces of arid-adapted animals that were able to survive in the desert and near-desert lands that then covered the rift valleys of Virginia.

Quite possibly there were nearby upland areas where other kinds of vertebrate life were still abundant. We see this situation today in the rift valley regions in the western United States, such as in New Mexico, Colorado, Nevada, and Utah. In those states, desert conditions prevail in most of the lowland areas where sediment is accumulating, but many adjacent upland areas have a much more diverse assemblage of animals. The Norian pollen record in the Culpeper Basin seems to hint at this, for the pollen record is far more diverse than the few kinds of plant remains found in the surviving dry lowland sedimentary deposits. If so, this is an example of a natural bias in the fossil record, which generally favors preservation of plants and animals that lived in the immediate environments in which the preserved strata were accumulating.

CHAPTER

5

LATE TRIASSIC, RHAETIAN:

THE CURTAIN CLOSES ON THE TRIASSIC WORLD

A bove the strata of the Passaic Formation, there is a prolonged missing interval of time, marked by an unconformity, during which sediment was not accumulating in the Virginia region. This unconformity included the upper part of the Norian stage and almost all of the following Rhaetian stage (Figure 2). This gap is present because the entirety of present-day eastern North America became somewhat uplifted at that time, causing both non-deposition and erosion to erase this time interval from the Virginia record. The source of this uplift was apparently the slow rise of a vast body of volcanic magma beneath an elongate zone that was in the process of becoming the Mid-Atlantic Ridge. It was not until these lava bodies began breaking through the land surface, rather like giant blisters bursting, that deposition resumed. In the exposed basins, this resumption of deposition only occurred in the western Newark Supergroup basins,[45] including the Culpeper Basin. In Virginia and elsewhere, dikes (long linear bodies of cooled magma that were once the feeder vents for these lava flows) are preserved throughout the Piedmont province and found even farther westward in parts of the Valley and Ridge region.[46] These rocks are also widespread beneath the Virginia Coastal Plain, but they are deeply buried and mostly inaccessible to study.

The upper Norian and Rhaetian time interval includes the youngest Triassic Land-Vertebrate Faunachron, called the Apachean (Figure 2). An abundant fauna of this age is known from the southwestern United States, but in the east only the oldest late Norian part of this faunachron is preserved in the stratigraphic record. It has yielded only conchostracans and a few sparse fossil footprints. A sliver of latest Rhaetian time, estimated to represent no more than a few tens of thousands of years,[47] is preserved in the Culpeper Basin above the Rhaetian unconformity. This interval, represented by the basal Partridge Island Member of the Talcott Formation, has not yielded any animal remains or footprints in Virginia, but it has yielded palynomorphs that indicate it is close in age to the Triassic-Jurassic boundary and much younger than the Norian strata that lie beneath the unconformity immediately below it.[48]

Above this basal sedimentary member, most of the rest of the Talcott Formation consists of basaltic lava flows. In the Culpeper Basin, the Mount Zion Old School Baptist Church historic site near Gilberts Corner in Loudoun County is a notable historic structure that was built upon the tilted erosional edge of the Talcott Basalt. The basalt is much more resistant to erosion than the sedimentary strata that lie immediately above and below it, so it forms a ridge that stands in relief to the surrounding lands. The volcanic episode that started with the massive series of Talcott basaltic flows spread thick layers of lava across much of central Pangaea. Remnants of these flows today spread all the way from Virginia into Nova Scotia and South Carolina, and eastward into Morocco, which then was directly adjacent to Virginia along its eastern margin.

Environmental changes and damage caused by the Talcott and equivalent flows climaxed a significant extinction event that was completed by the end of the Triassic Period. This extinction was once thought to have resulted from a single catastrophic event that occurred at the very end of the Triassic, but newer and more detailed analysis has shown that it was actually an event of longer duration, called a "step-wise" extinction.[49] Although not so devastating as the Great End-Permian Extinction Event, the Late Triassic extinction event still killed off at least half of the species then living. Throughout the world, not just in the eastern United States, procolophonids, rauisuchians, phytosaurs, and aetosaurs became extinct by the time the Talcott event was finished, as well as most species of the larger amphibians and mammal-like reptiles.

Two subsequent major eruption events produced the Holyoke and Hampden flows. These flows, although quite large and voluminous (Figure 2), apparently did not cause any further major extinctions based on the fossils found between and above them. Therefore, it seems that nearly all of the extinctions in the terrestrial environments were over by the time the Talcott flows began to cool. By the time the Talcott flows ended, the Mesozoic world had been significantly reorganized, and a new global ecosystem had been established that heralded the beginning of the Jurassic world.

CHAPTER

6

EARLY JURASSIC, HETTANGIAN:

THE DAWN OF THE JURASSIC WORLD

After a prolonged period of erosion in eastern North America during the latter part of the Norian and most of the Rhaetian, deposition resumed in the western Newark Supergroup rift valleys in the latest Rhaetian, and continued through the Hettangian and into the early part of the subsequent Sinemurian stage (Figure 2). In Virginia, only latest Rhaetian and Hettangian strata remain. Farther northeast, in Connecticut and Massachusetts, younger strata survive that continue the story somewhat further into the Jurassic. Newark Supergroup strata deposited from the latest Rhaetian of the Triassic through the first half of the Hettangian stage of the Jurassic are collected into a stratigraphic sequence called the Meriden Group, which is lithologically different from the underlying Triassic sequence named the Chatham Group. This is because of the huge volume of basaltic lavas in strata above the Chatham Group, which gives the Meriden Group a very different character than the beds below (Figure 2).

The Meriden Group is characterized by an abundance of volcanic rocks, mostly in the form of basaltic lava flows, but also, rarely, as volcanic ash materials. Interbedded with these volcanic rocks, sedimentary units provide the only remaining Early Jurassic record of life in the Virginia region. These strata are found in only a few of the westernmost exposed rift valleys that had formed earlier during the Triassic Period. Apparently, by the end of the Triassic, the more easterly basins had ceased to be geologically active.[45] In Virginia, the only basin that contains Meriden Group strata is the Culpeper Basin in northern Virginia. The age of the Meriden Group has been established by conchostracan biozones,[4] and this is supported by biostratigraphy based on pollen recovered from these same beds. Its age is also supported by vertebrate remains, which are typical examples of the earliest Jurassic Wassonian Land-Vertebrate

Faunachron, first recognized and established in the western United States (Figure 2).

The Virginia region had continued its northward drift until, by the Hettangian stage of the Jurassic, it was near the northern edge of the northern low latitude desert belt. As a result, the regional climate was becoming less arid and better vegetated. This is partly reflected in the Early Jurassic fish fauna, which not only is more diverse and abundant than it had been in the early and middle Norian, but also included larger fish, indicating abundant water and a climate that did not undergo prolonged seasonal droughts on a regular basis. Five species of bony fishes have been found (Figure 14, Table 1) that belong to three genera: *Redfieldius*, *Semionotus*, and *Ptycholepis*. The small Triassic lobe-finned fish *Diplurus newarki* was gone, but its much larger relative, *Diplurus longicaudatus*, continued to exist.[50]

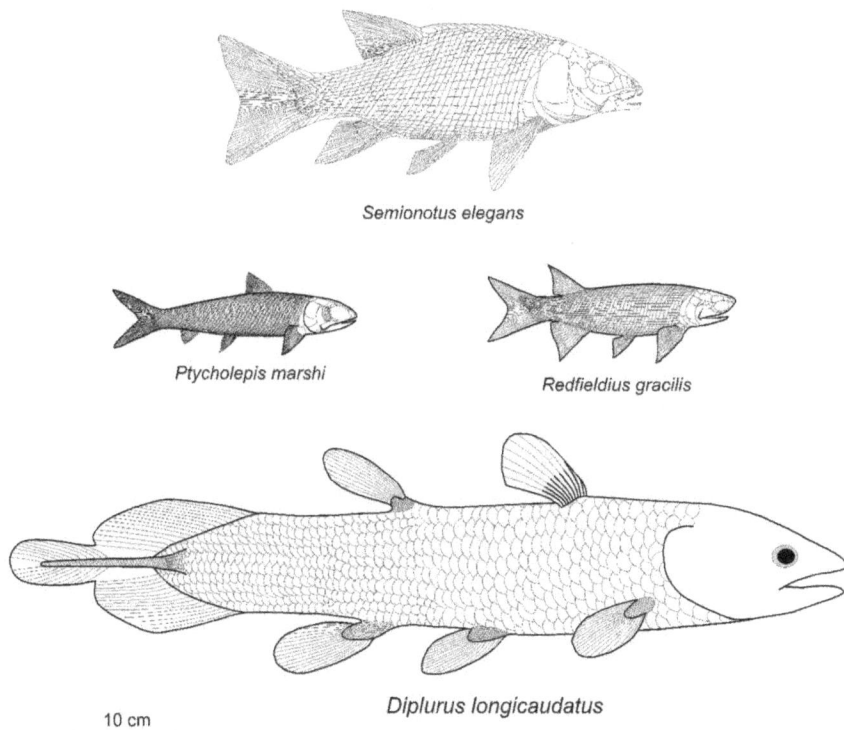

Semionotus elegans

Ptycholepis marshi

Redfieldius gracilis

10 cm

Diplurus longicaudatus

Figure 14 – Typical Wassonian freshwater fishes known from the Hettangian of Virginia. Sources for figure shown in Appendix 2.

The Hettangian was the beginning of the Jurassic Period, and as befits an opening act, it set the stage for what was to follow throughout the remainder of the Jurassic. Notably missing at the beginning of the Jurassic were the host of archosaur reptiles, which had all vanished by the end of the Triassic except for a single lineage that gave rise to the modern crocodilians. This crocodile lineage is represented in Virginia by small footprints called *Batrachopus*, which were probably made by the primitive crocodilian *Protosuchus*. In striking contrast, all of the major groups

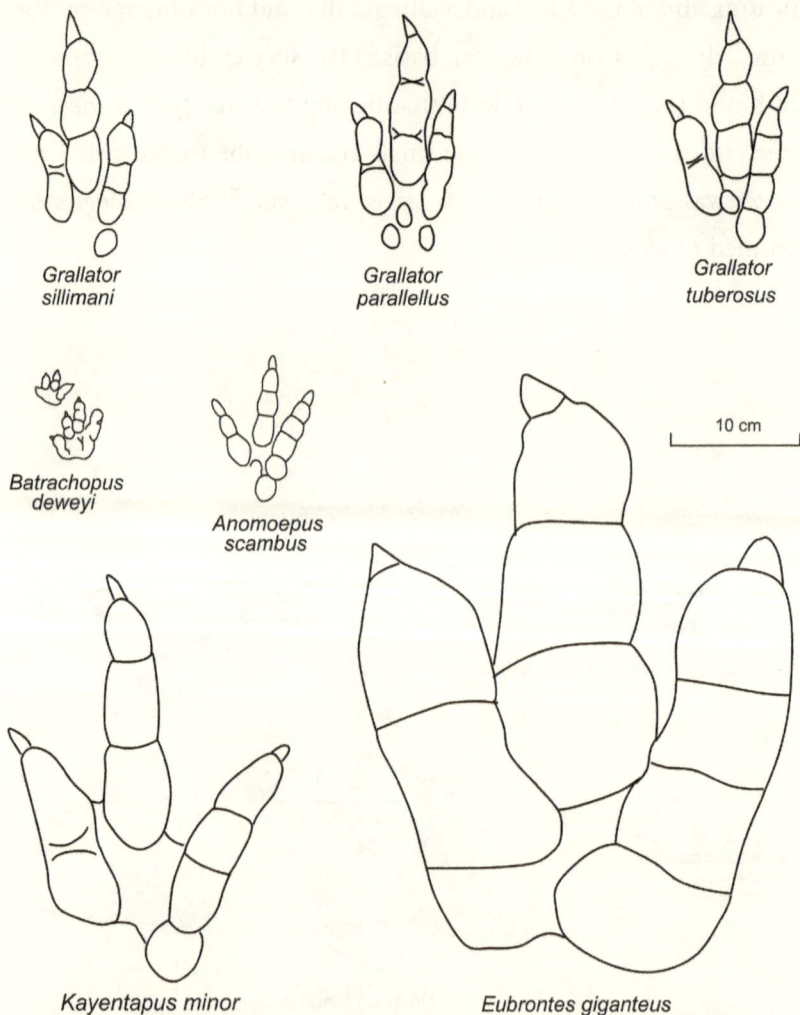

Figure 15 – Typical Wassonian footprints known from the Hettangian of Virginia. Source for figure shown in Appendix 2.

of dinosaurs that had been present at the end of the Triassic (theropods, sauropods, and ornithischians) survived the Triassic-Jurassic extinction and were becoming generally larger. This tendency continued to characterize dinosaur groups throughout the remainder of the Jurassic. In Virginia, the only evidence so far for Early Jurassic dinosaurs consists of numerous footprints, which show that they were abundant and diverse here.

As elsewhere within the Newark Supergroup, the largest and most abundant animals in this fauna were prosauropods, which made footprints called *Eubrontes*. These three-toed footprints were once considered to be those of carnivorous theropod dinosaurs, but a mounting body of evidence shows that they are instead footprints of herbivores of large size that roamed the Early Jurassic landscape in great numbers. The animals that made the other Early Jurassic dinosaur tracks have not been positively identified, but the *Eubrontes* trackmaker was almost certainly the prosauropod dinosaur *Anchisaurus*, which is known from skeletal material found in the Hartford Basin in Massachusetts and the Fundy Basin in Nova Scotia.[51] Found elsewhere in the Early Jurassic Newark Supergroup, but so far not found in Virginia, are footprints of another early sauropodomorph dinosaur called *Otozoum*. Unlike the *Eubrontes* trackmaker, which was fully bipedal and almost never walked on its front legs, the *Otozoum* trackmaker frequently dropped onto its front legs to walk and was in the process of returning to a permanently four-footed pose. This animal belonged to the sauropod lineage that gave rise to the giant sauropod dinosaurs of the later Jurassic and the Cretaceous. In contrast, the *Eubrontes* trackmakers, even though they were very successful for a while, were part of a line that was destined to die out by the end of the Early Jurassic.

In the Hettangian, footprints of ornithischian dinosaurs are abundant but small. They represent a variety of types, however, hinting that this group was beginning to radiate into the diverse types of herbivorous dinosaurs that later became such a prominent part of the northern hemisphere dinosaur faunas in the Cretaceous Period.

The principal predators in this Early Jurassic world were theropod dinosaurs. They came in distinctly smaller and larger size classes. The smaller group included the same three ichnospecies of *Grallator* that were present in the latest Triassic. The small bird-like track *Plesiornis pilulatus* has not been found yet in the Virginia Jurassic, but it is known from beds of similar age in Connecticut and Massachusetts, so it is likely that these tracks will eventually be found here as well.

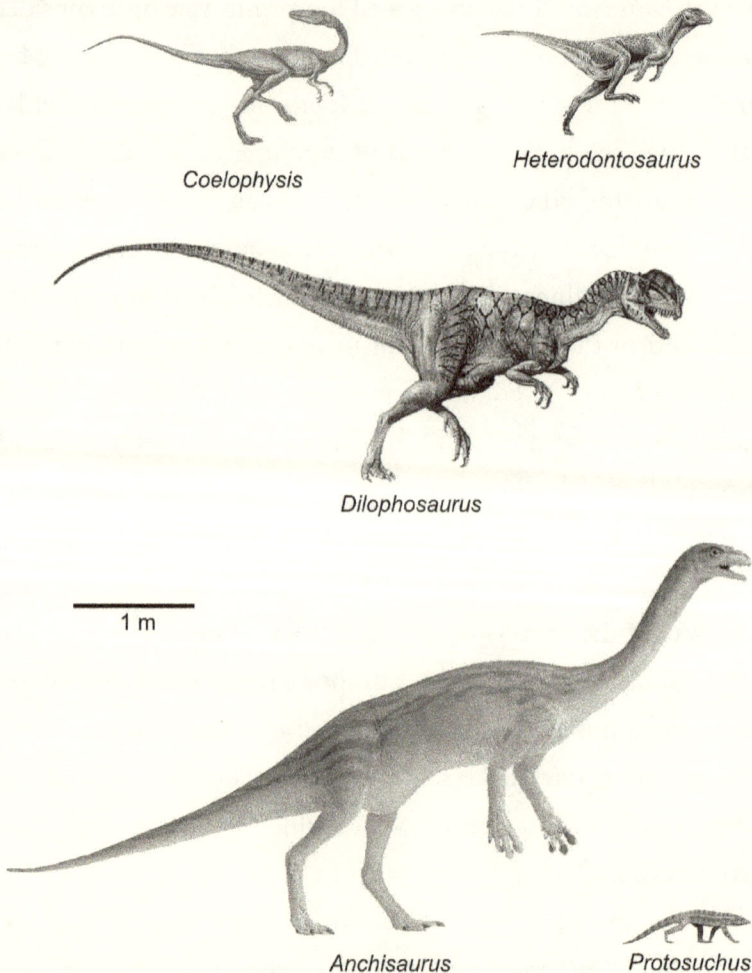

Figure 16 – Possible trackmakers of the Wassonian footprints found in the Hettangian of Virginia. Sources for figure shown in Appendix 2.

Large predator tracks also come in two distinctly different types, indicating that there were two kinds of large carnivores. One was the *Kayentapus* track-maker, which had somewhat increased in size from its Triassic antecedents and continued to hunt prey in Virginia. In the Deerfield and Hartford basins in the Connecticut Valley, but so far not in Virginia, a new and different kind of predator footprint had appeared called *Gigandipus*. It was somewhat larger than the *Kayentapus* track-maker based on its foot size, and it is interesting to speculate on how these two large apex carnivores coexisted in the same region. Possibly the *Kayentapus* trackmaker, which may well have been the ancestor of the slightly younger Early Jurassic dinosaur *Dilophosaurus*, primarily hunted the prosauropod *Anchisaurus*, which was the *Eubrontes* track-maker. The *Gigandipus* trackmaker instead may have been the principal predator of the *Otozoum* track-maker, which was somewhat larger than the *Eubrontes* track-maker and a member of the line of dinosaurs that evolved into the true sauropods of the later Jurassic and Cretaceous.

The land vertebrate fauna of the Lower Jurassic Meriden Group in Virginia belongs to the Wassonian Land-Vertebrate Faunachron, named from the fauna found in the oldest Jurassic rocks exposed on the Colorado Plateau in the southwestern United States.[9] The Hettangian fauna known from Virginia is not as diverse as the namesake Wassonian fauna from the western United States, but this is almost certainly due to the fact that there is very limited exposure of Meriden sedimentary strata in Virginia, which therefore offer very limited outcrops to be explored. To the north, a far more diverse vertebrate fauna of this age has been collected from the Fundy Basin in Nova Scotia, Canada, which includes bones and teeth of a number of small reptiles and primitive mammals.[52] Most or all of these animals probably existed here in Hettangian time, but their remains are yet to be discovered.

CHAPTER

7

THE "GREAT HIATUS" IN THE STRATIGRAPHIC RECORD OF EASTERN NORTH AMERICA

The fossil record of the Jurassic Period in Virginia ends slightly before the end of the Hettangian stage. Higher beds of the Newark Supergroup were probably once present here, but they have long since been eroded away. The highest beds remaining anywhere in the Newark Supergroup of eastern America are found in the Hartford and Deerfield basins of Connecticut and Massachusetts. These beds have yielded remains showing that little changed in the fauna of the eastern United States region at least until the middle of the succeeding Sinemurian stage (Figure 2). In the western United States, the much better-preserved Jurassic record there shows a significant faunal turnover at about the middle of the Sinemurian stage. It seems likely that this faunal turnover happened in the east as well, but on this the eastern American record is silent. After the early part of the Sinemurian, there is no available stratigraphic record for the next eighty million years that is preserved near the land surface in the eastern United States.

By the end of the Sinemurian stage of the Early Jurassic (Figure 2), it is likely that the opening of the Atlantic Ocean Basin had begun in earnest. The exact timing of this event is somewhat difficult to pin down because its record is now deeply buried beneath the sea far east of the present Virginia shoreline. From near the base of very deep oil prospect wells off Newfoundland in Canada and at Cape Hatteras in North Carolina, sediment samples have been recovered. These indicate that by the Late Jurassic, sediment was beginning to accumulate along the edge of the continental shelf of the newly formed continent of North America, including Virginia.[53] This oceanic repository for sediment has continued to accumulate strata through the present day, creating a detailed record of the last 160 million years. But, because this record is deeply buried and located far offshore of the present Virginia coastline, it remains for all practical purposes inaccessible. It is not until the later part of the Early Cretaceous, around 110 million years ago, that deposition along the American Eastern Seaboard advanced westward far enough to lay down strata along the western margin of the Virginia Coastal Plain that are accessible for study today.

We can gain some idea of what must have been happening on land in the later Jurassic here in eastern North America from Upper Jurassic strata located in the western United States about 1,500 miles west of Virginia. There, abundant skeletal remains from these strata have been collected and studied for almost 150 years. Similarly, there is also knowledge to be gained from marine strata located about one thousand miles to our south, exposed in the mountains of western Cuba. As distant as these places are from Virginia, they are where the closest accessible Late Jurassic deposits can be found, and therefore they likely had faunas similar to the one that once existed here (Figure 17).

The very productive Late Jurassic fossil beds of the Morrison Formation,[54] particularly in Colorado, Wyoming, and Utah, have yielded a diverse terrestrial fauna that shows the herbivorous sauropods had continued to increase in size and diversified into a number of different families. These came in two distinctly different body plans. One type, represented in the Morrison by *Diplodocus* and *Camarasaurus*, had necks elongated to search for food on and near the ground. They might be thought of as giant vacuum cleaners, sweeping back and forth across the earth as they walked along, searching for fallen fruits and nuts, or any sprouting vegetation that could be bitten off and swallowed. The other group, represented by *Brachiosaurus*, had upwardly arched necks and forelegs that were elongated to graze high in trees much like modern giraffes. By grazing high in the treetops, they avoided competing for food with the low browsing sauropods and the ornithischians. Because of their small mouths and nipping teeth, none of these animals were designed for chewing. Instead, all of these types of sauropods must have simply gathered food and swallowed it, leaving the job of digesting this material to their stomachs and intestines.

The ornithischians, which had been small and generalized in the Hettangian, had greatly diversified through the course of the Jurassic and become far more abundant than they had been during the Hettangian. Semi-bipedal ornithopods had appeared, such as *Camptosaurus*. A quint-essential dinosaur group, the stegosaurs with their bizarre armor plating were in their heyday in the Late Jurassic (Figure 18). Stegosaurs persisted into the Early Cretaceous, but then died out and were gone by the time the Virginia Mesozoic fossil record begins again. Other armored forms, relatively rare in the Late Jurassic Morrison Formation, lived alongside the stegosaurs and gave rise to the armored tank-like ankylosaurian dino-saurs of the Cretaceous.

Small carnivorous dinosaurs were represented by such forms as *Coe-lurus* and *Ornitholestes*. Although so far unknown from North America, a number of small, feathered bird-like species of this age have been de-scribed from China and Europe.

Another interesting theropod group that appeared by this time were the tyrannosaurs, represented in the Morrison by *Stokesaurus*. In the Late Jurassic, tyrannosaurs were still small predators that could not have com-peted with the top predators of the Jurassic world. Those apex predator roles were held by *Ceratosaurus*, which may have been descended from dinosaurs that made *Kayentapus* tracks, and *Allosaurus* and *Torvosaurus*, either or both of which may have been descended from the group of dinosaurs that made the *Gigandipus* tracks found in the Hettangian. *Cer-atosaurus* seems to have disappeared from North America by the Early Cretaceous, but the other groups of large carnivorous dinosaurs contin-ued into the Early Cretaceous relatively unchanged.

Late Jurassic marine strata are found to our south in western Cuba. [55] These marine beds give us a glimpse of what marine life must have been like in what was then the narrow infant Jurassic Atlantic Ocean off

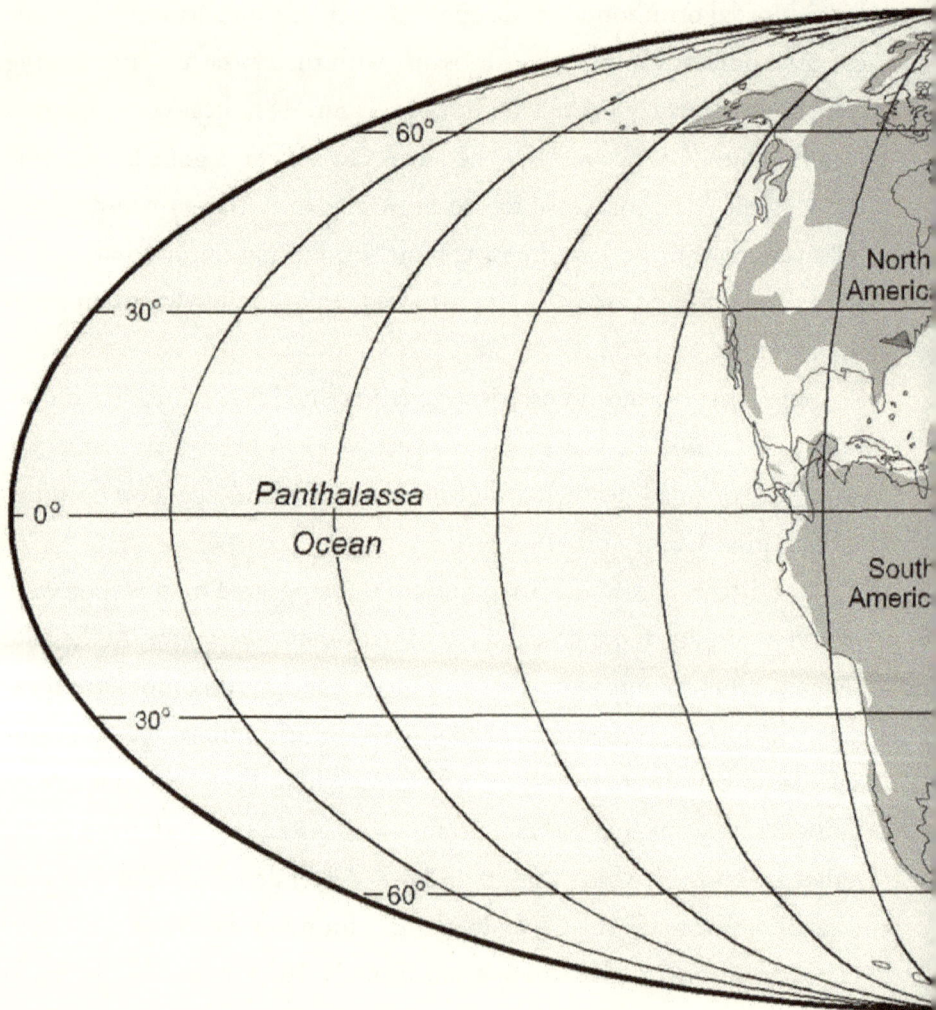

60°

North
America

30°

0°

Panthalassa
Ocean

South
America

30°

60°

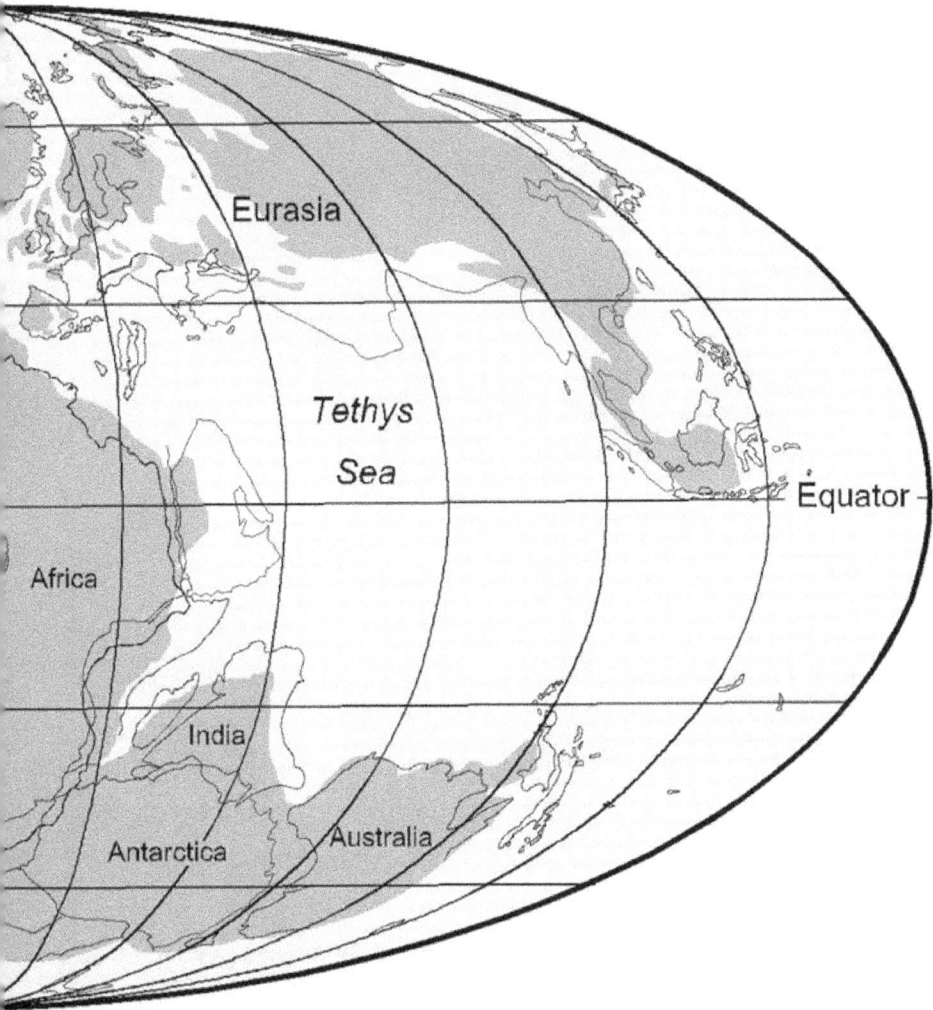

Figure 17 – Distribution of continents during the Late Jurassic. Location of Virginia indicated by dark shaded region. Source for figure shown in Appendix 2.

Figure 18 - *Characteristic Late Jurassic dinosaurs known from the western United States. Sources for figure shown in Appendix 2.*

the east coast of Virginia. Remains of diverse Late Jurassic marine bony fishes are common, but also present are remains of marine-going reptiles including plesiosaurs, pliosaurs, crocodilians, pleurodire (side-neck) turtles, and ichthyosaurs (Figure 19).

Also present are remains of rhamphorhynchid pterosaurs, which, like modern sea birds, probably ranged far out to sea in search of fish. A metacarpal bone of a camarasaurid sauropod dinosaur has been found in Cuba that probably came from a bloated sauropod carcass that washed out to sea. This exceptional discovery offers hope that more dinosaur remains may yet be recovered from these deposits.

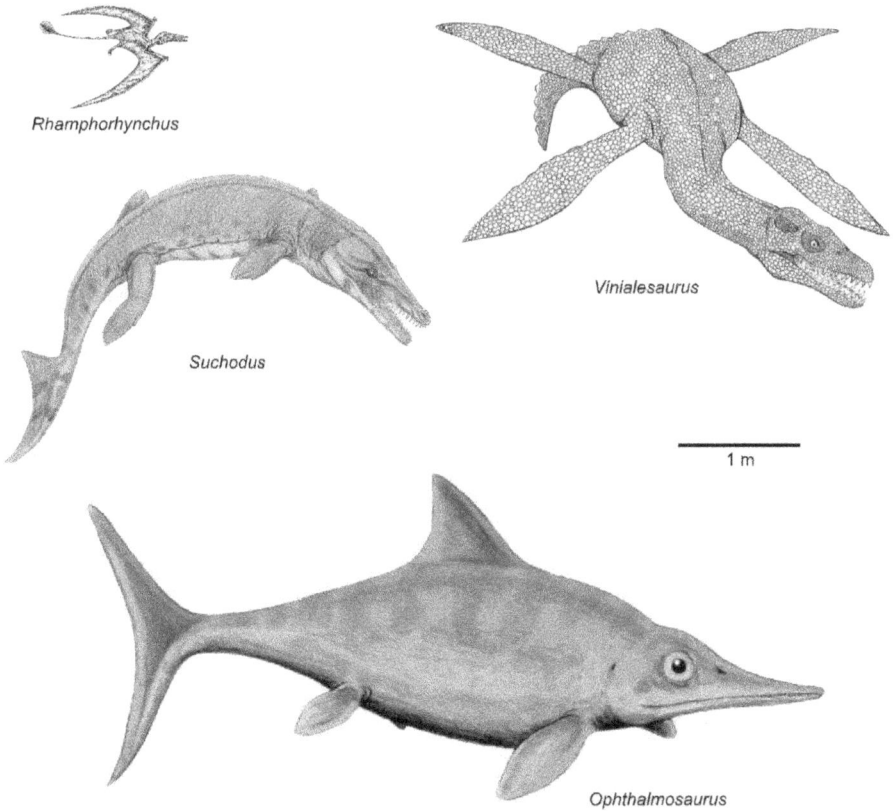

Figure 19 - Characteristic Late Jurassic marine reptiles and the pterosaur Rhamphorhynchus known from Cuba. Sources for figure shown in Appendix 2.

Although the Colorado deposits give us a general sense of what sorts of Late Jurassic dinosaurs probably lived in Virginia, and the Cuban deposits give us a general sense of what sorts of fish and marine reptiles lived in the newly formed North Atlantic sea off of Virginia's eastern coast, there seems little or no prospect that any remains from the Middle or Late Jurassic will ever be found in the Virginia area to fill in this gap locally. If the offshore Jurassic deposits are ever explored by deep wells, it is likely that we can gain some idea from pollen and spores as to what the vegetation was like in this area during the Late Jurassic. Similarly, the chemistry and mineralogy of any Late Jurassic sediment samples recovered in the future may give us some strong clues as to what the climate was like during that time. But despite these possible future discoveries, the identity of the Late Jurassic Virginia dinosaurs and marine reptiles that lived here will probably always remain a mystery whose answers are lost in time.

CHAPTER

8

EARLY CRETACEOUS, EARLY ALBIAN:

THE APEX OF THE AGE OF DINOSAURS IN VIRGINIA

The great gap in the accessible Mesozoic record in Virginia continued through at least the first half of the Early Cretaceous (Figure 2). Then, a major regional tectonic reorganization of the greater Atlantic Basin altered this situation dramatically. Although the North Atlantic and South Atlantic oceans today seem like a single feature, they had rather different origins and very different early histories. The South Atlantic Basin began to form about fifty million years later than the North Atlantic Basin, and the events that created it were intimately linked with an age-equivalent tectonic reorganization in the North Atlantic and Caribbean basins. One result was that the eastern margin of North America, including eastern Virginia, began to subside across a much wider area than before. Prior to the middle of the Early Cretaceous, subsidence and deposition along the eastern margin of Virginia was confined to what is more or less the modern Virginia offshore continental shelf. But once the South Atlantic sea floor formed and began to spread, the area experiencing subsidence along the eastern margin of Virginia expanded substantially to the west of the present coastline to form what we now call the Virginia Coastal Plain.

The western margin of the Virginia Coastal Plain is defined by a major north-south trending fault-system, marked today by the trace of the Tidewater Fall Line and Interstate Highway 95.[5] West of this fault line uplift, erosion, and eastward transport of sediment began filling the vast new lowland area situated to the east of the fault line with Lower Cretaceous sediment (Figure 3). The earliest sediments deposited to the east of this east-facing fault system were coarse sands and gravels that accumulated as a series of coalescing alluvial fans. The sediment in these fans constitutes most of the western outcrop region of the Patuxent Formation in Virginia. This is the only Cretaceous unit widely exposed today in this area,[56] though on the Quantico Marine base just west of the Potomac River estuary and at a place on the James River near Dutch Gap, remnants of a second somewhat younger Lower Cretaceous unit called the Patapsco Formation are locally preserved above the Patuxent (Figure 2). These two areas have yielded a very informative suite of plant remains,[57] but no vertebrate material has been found. The Arundel Formation, a third Lower Cretaceous unit that lies stratigraphically between these two formations, is present in Maryland but not in Virginia. Whether the Arundel is a variant facies of the Patuxent or a separate unit lying unconformably between the Patuxent and Patapsco is a question that remains unresolved.[58]

As was true in earlier Mesozoic times, the drift of North America northward and westward continued throughout the time interval now lost in the great mid-Mesozoic unconformity. This meant that, by the later Early Cretaceous, Virginia and Maryland had drifted northward to about thirty degrees north latitude and lay beyond the north-latitude desert climatic belt where they had previously been located. Today, this is about the same latitude as northern Florida. The paleogeography of North America is shown in Figure 20 as it was during the early Albian stage of the Early Cretaceous. The general appearance of the continent is largely recognizable except for the presence of an elongate inland sea that stretched down from the Arctic Ocean into Colorado and Utah.

The climate in Virginia during Patuxent time was apparently monsoonal.[59] Prolonged dry spells would end with rainy seasons, accompanied by flooding and rapid eastward transport of Piedmont rock debris and soil. This material was deposited in the western Coastal Plain by braided streams, which are characteristic of high-flow and steep gradient river systems. Once the rainy season was over, the sediments that had just been deposited sat through the dry season and baked. Dinosaur footprints made on top of these flood-deposited sediments soon after the high flood waters receded became hardened during the dry season.

They would be preserved until the next rainy season, when renewed rains deposited more sediment on top of them. These braided stream deposits formed mostly within twenty miles of the western margin of the Virginia Coastal Plain, adjacent to the Tidewater Fall Line. Farther toward the east, the braided streams lost energy and discharged their waters onto the coastal flats adjacent to the westward encroaching Early Cretaceous Atlantic Ocean. At Oak Grove in Westmoreland County, Virginia, located about thirty miles east of the Tidewater Fall Line, a deep core encountered the mineral glauconite at the top of the Patuxent interval.[60] This mineral forms only on the sea floor, and its presence clearly indicates that the Early Cretaceous Atlantic Ocean at least briefly encroached across the central Virginia Coastal Plain to within thirty miles of the present-day Tidewater Fall Line.

North of Aquia Creek in Virginia, later faulting uplifted the western edge of the Patuxent Formation and eroded it away.[61] As a result the very coarse sediments are gone that formed north of Aquia Creek and just east of the Tidewater Fall Line in Early Cretaceous time. This erosion has exposed strata in Maryland that still remain deeply buried in Virginia and are thus inaccessible. This explains why the outcropping Patuxent Formation strata in Maryland are much finer-grained than the age-equivalent Patuxent strata that are exposed in Virginia, and why those strata have yielded far more skeletal remains of Early Cretaceous animals than have the Patuxent strata in Virginia.

The Patuxent Formation in Virginia has yielded abundant remains of plants that lived at that time. Besides pollen, spores, and leaf impressions, petrified trunks of large trees are commonly found that belong to extinct coniferous species related to Norfolk Island pines, redwoods, and cypresses. Abundant petrified wood from smaller understory plants, such as cycadeoids, tree ferns, and true ferns, are also present. Only about six primitive species of shrubby flowering plants have been identified in the early Albian Patuxent Formation, and none of them are especially com-

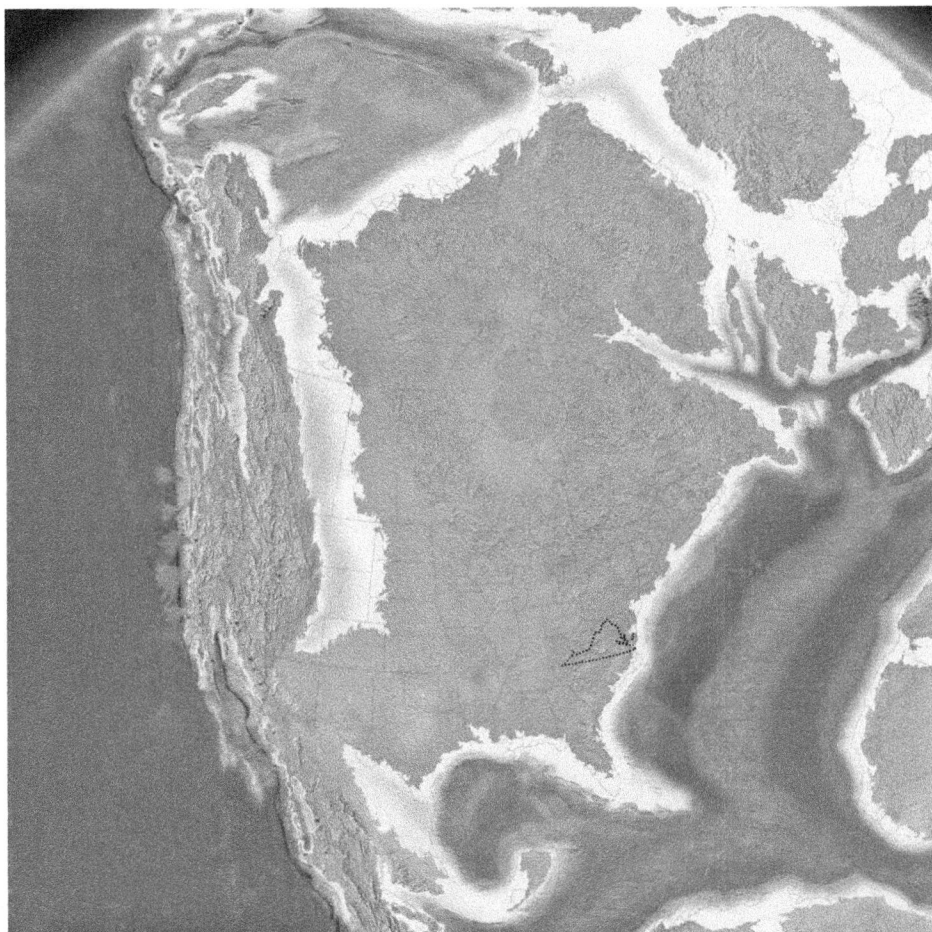

Figure 20 – The paleogeography of North America in the early Albian stage of the Cretaceous. Location of Virginia indicated by dashed lines. Sources for figure shown in Appendix 2.

mon.[62] By the time the overlying Patapsco Formation was deposited later in the Albian, angiosperm diversity had increased considerably to about 22 species.[63] In Patuxent time, however, flowering plants were still quite rare, and the Patuxent-Arundel fauna and flora remained much as it had been during the mid-Mesozoic times that are missing from our exposed regional Mesozoic record.

The vertebrate fauna from the Early Cretaceous of Virginia and Maryland includes a number of fish (Figure 21). The one Patuxent Formation fish known from Virginia is a single impression of a freshwater bony fish similar or identical to the genus *Paraelops*.[64] Deposits from

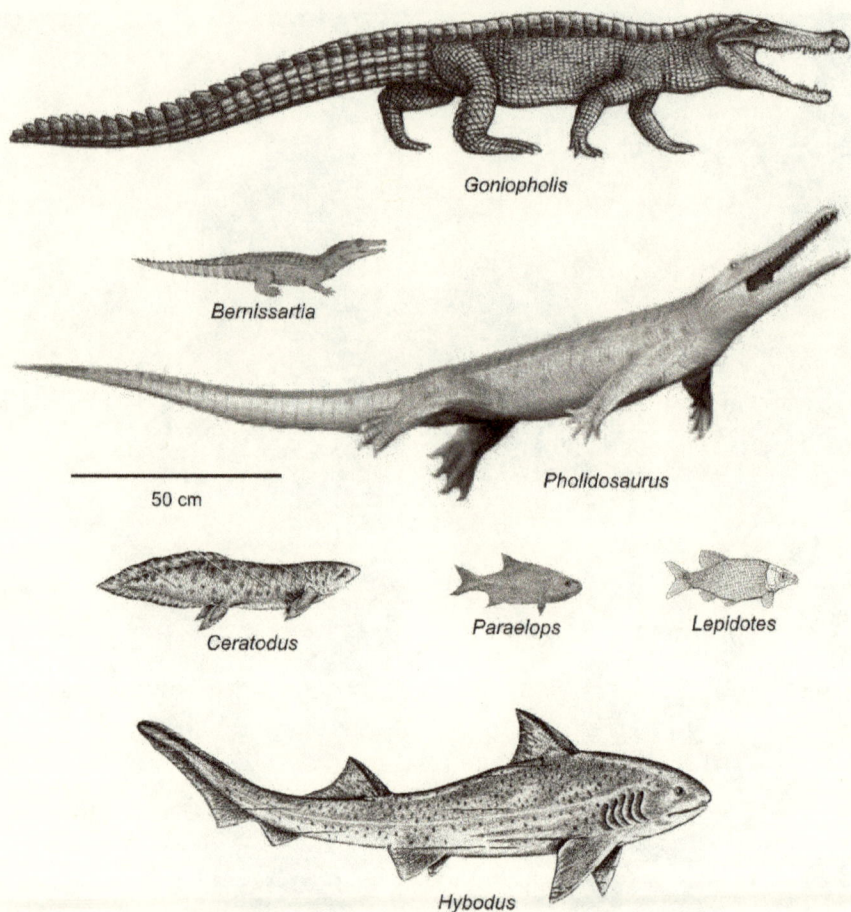

Figure 21 – Freshwater reptiles and fishes known from the early Aptian stage in Maryland and Virginia. The crocodilians shown represent the three families known from Maryland, which are not yet identifiable at a generic level. Sources for figure shown in Appendix 2.

the Maryland Arundel Formation contain more abundant fish remains, including another bony fish named *Lepidotes*; teeth of two kinds of freshwater shark, *Hybodus* and *Egertonodus*; and a lungfish named *Ceratodus*.[65]

Among lower land vertebrates, footprints of a frog and those of a turtle have been found in the Patuxent Formation in Virginia.[66] More informative are skeletal remains of turtles found in the Maryland Arundel Formation that can specifically be assigned to the genera *Arundelemys*, *Glyptops*, and *Naomichelys*.[67] Crocodilian skeletal remains also are found in the Arundel. None of these so far can be identified to a genus or species level, but they are complete enough to show that they belong to at least three different families of crocodilians.[68] This indicates that crocodilians had greatly recovered from the end-Triassic extinction event and were becoming diverse again. Footprints of pterosaurs have been found in the Patuxent Formation in Maryland, and these have been referred to the ichnogenus *Pteraichnus*.[69] These footprints document the presence of at least one kind of pterosaur in the Early Cretaceous fauna of the Maryland-Virginia region.

Most abundant in the Patuxent and Arundel formations are footprints and skeletal remains of dinosaurs (Figures 22-24). Thirteen types have been recognized. The largest of these dinosaurs was a sauropod, known from bones and teeth in Maryland and described from there as *Astrodon johnstoni*.[70] In Virginia and Maryland, sauropod footprints probably made by this same kind of animal have been referred to the footprint taxon *Brontopodus*.[71] *Astrodon* was a brachiosaurid sauropod with a long and upwardly directed neck, which indicates that it browsed for food among the treetops. Remains of juvenile animals are most commonly found, but the largest adult bones and the larger footprints indicate that *Astrodon* grew to a length of about seventy feet. This is by far the largest dinosaur known from the Virginia region. It is not so large, however, as the truly gigantic sauropods that lived in North America in the Late Jurassic, such as *Brachiosaurus*, *Diplodocus*, and *Supersaurus*.[72]

The single species of sauropod known from the Early Cretaceous of Virginia and Maryland stands in striking contrast to the great diversity of sauropods documented from the Late Jurassic Morrison Formation of the Rocky Mountains region, where a total of 13 genera are known. Sauropod diversity in North America sharply declined during the Early Cretaceous, but even so, at about the same time that the Patuxent and Arundel formations were accumulating, three sauropod genera were present in Texas and Oklahoma.[73] This suggests that North American sauropod diversity had not only declined greatly in the Early Cretaceous throughout North America, but that there was also a strong decline in diversity northward, away from the equator. This implies that *Astrodon* was living near the northern range limit for Early Cretaceous sauropods, and that sauropods as a group had a strong preference for equatorial climates. Even so, the abundant juvenile bones, teeth, and footprints of *Astrodon* demonstrate that at least this genus of sauropod was successfully reproducing and rearing young in the Virginia region during the Early Cretaceous. Evidently, it was fully adapted to its local climate.

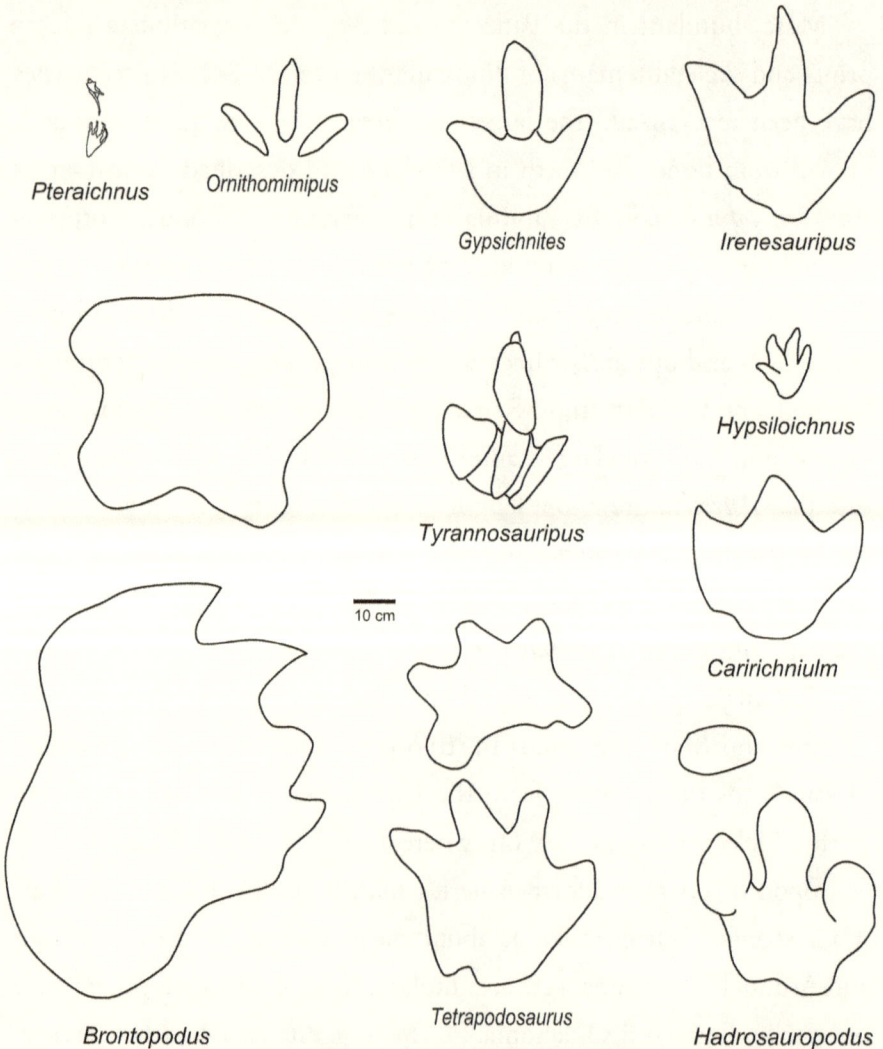

Figure 22 – Outlines of fossil dinosaur and pterosaur (Pteraichnus) footprints known from the early Albian stage in Maryland and Virginia. Source for figure shown in Appendix 2.

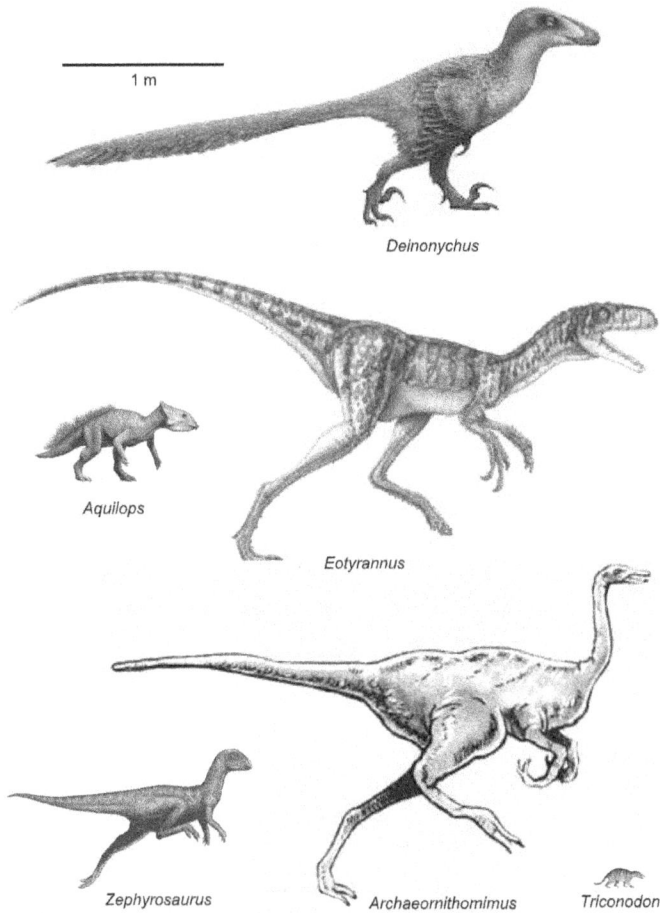

Figure 23 – Small dinosaurs and a mammal (Triconodon) known from the early Albian stage in Maryland. Sources for figure shown in Appendix 2.

Toward the end of the Early Cretaceous, ornithischian dinosaurs had become much more diverse in Maryland and Virginia, while sauropod diversity was declining. Ornithischians strongly dominated the ground-level herbivore niches that had been dominated by the low browsing diplodocid and camarasaurid sauropods in the Late Jurassic. Those animals were gone, leaving understory environments almost entirely to the ornithischians. Of these, bipedal to semi-bipedal ornithischians were the most common and diverse. Footprints named *Hypsiloichnus* document the presence of a very small ornithischian dinosaur in both

Maryland and Virginia. Being an herbivore of small size, it was likely very abundant and secretive, rather like deer are today. Its trackmaker may have been *Zephyrosaurus* (Figure 23), known from the age-equivalent Cloverly Formation in Montana.[74]

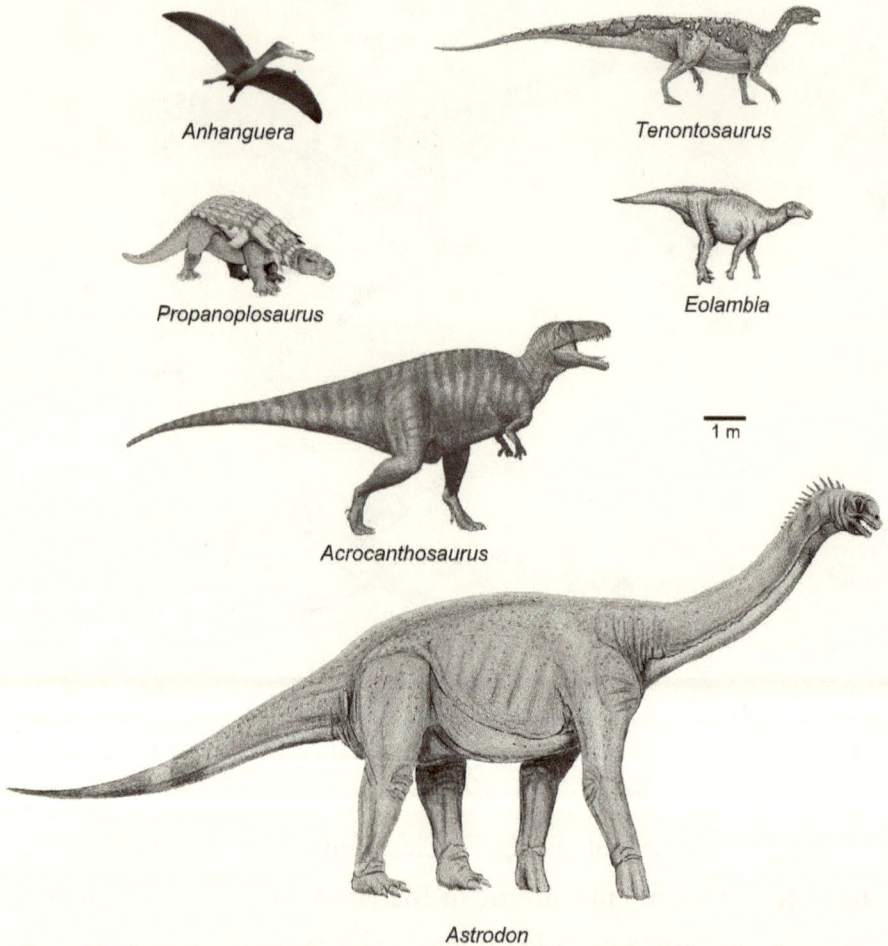

Anhanguera

Tenontosaurus

Propanoplosaurus

Eolambia

1 m

Acrocanthosaurus

Astrodon

Figure 24 – Large dinosaurs and a pterosaur (Anhanguera) known from the early Albian stage in Maryland and Virginia. Sources for figure shown in Appendix 2.

Larger bipedal to semi-bipedal ornithischian forms are documented by the footprint taxa *Caririchnium* and *Hadrosauropodus*.[75] *Caririchnium* tracks were likely made by an iguanodontid dinosaur similar to the skeletal dinosaur genus *Tenontosaurus*, teeth of which have been reported from the Maryland Arundel Formation.[74] Iguanodontids were the dominant mid-size herbivores in North America throughout most of the Early Cretaceous. Their footprints have been documented in Virginia in clusters all heading in the same direction, indicating that they often moved in herds. Non-iguanodontid footprints named *Hadrosauropodus* more rarely are found in the Patuxent Formation.[75] They were almost certainly made by a primitive hadrosaurid dinosaur similar to *Eolambia* (Figure 24). In the Late Cretaceous, the iguanodontids became extinct and were replaced by the hadrosaurids. In the late Early Cretaceous footprint fauna of Virginia and Maryland, we see the beginning stages of this turnover and replacement.

Besides bipedal ornithischians, two groups of fully quadrupedal ornithischians are represented. The more abundant of these were nodosaurid ankylosaurs, which were tank-like herbivores with heavily armored backs and spikes along the outer edges of their armor (Figure 24). Their footprints are abundant in the Patuxent of Virginia and assigned to the ichnogenus *Tetrapodosaurus*.[75] In Maryland, a partial skeleton has been found of a juvenile of this type of animal that has been named *Proplanoprosaurus marylandicus*.[76] Also present in Maryland are fragmentary remains of a neoceratopsian dinosaur that is closely related to the ancestral group from which later horned ceratopsian dinosaurs arose.[77] This animal was probably very closely related to *Aquilops*, known from the nearly age-equivalent Cloverly Formation of Montana (Figure 23).

Among theropod dinosaurs, the top carnivore at that time was *Acrocanthosaurus*, known from teeth found in Maryland.[78] *Acrocanthosaurus* belonged to a family of carnivorous dinosaurs known as carcharodontosaurids, which were the apex predators throughout most of the world during the Early Cretaceous. This animal was likely the main predator on the large sauropod dinosaur *Astrodon*, though it surely would have opportunistically grabbed unwary smaller animals as well. Footprints of a large predator, called *Irenesauripus* (Figure 22), have been found in Virginia, and these probably pertain to *Acrocanthosaurus*.[79] A somewhat smaller theropod footprint found in Virginia has been referred to a new ichnotaxon, *Tyrannosauripus bachmani.*[80] It was made by an early tyran-nosaurid dinosaur similar to *Eotyrannus*, known from skeletal material found in the Early Cretaceous of England (Figure 23). This animal, based on its relatively small size, was clearly not a direct competitor with the larger theropods. It was, however, in the right size range to hunt many of the medium and small ornithopod dinosaurs in this fauna. Another medium-size predator is represented by footprints called *Gypsichnites*. In the past, these tracks were considered to be ornithischian footprints, but current thinking is that they were made by some kind of theropod. No skeletal taxon can be matched to this kind of track at present, so the exact nature of the animal that made it remains elusive.[80] Teeth of a still small-er kind of predator named *Deinonychus* have been found in Maryland. [68] Although small by dinosaur standards, *Deinonychus* likely hunted in groups. These animals were surely vicious predators based on the very sharp and long claws they possessed.[81]

Skeletal remains of another theropod group have also been found in the Arundel Formation in Maryland, though these animals were not as strongly adapted to predation as were other members of this group. These were ornithomimosaurs, or ostrich-mimic dinosaurs. Although they cannot as yet be identified to a particular genus or species, at least two different types of these animals were present.[82] A footprint, probably made by one kind of these animals, was found in Virginia and referred to the footprint ichnotaxon *Ornithomimipus angustens.*[75] This animal, based on its body build and leg anatomy, was almost certainly a very fast runner. As its name suggests, it was rather similar in its appearance and habits to the ostriches of today. More recently, a second kind of smaller ornithomimid track has been identified in Virginia and assigned to the footprint ichnotaxon *Ornithomimipus jaillardi.*[80]

The outcrop areas of the Patuxent and Arundel formations in Vir-ginia and Maryland are restricted, and this has left us with only a limited fauna from strata of this age. Even so, the Patuxent-Arundel fauna is strikingly similar to two better-known faunas of about the same age found in the western United States, the Paluxy Formation fauna in Texas and the Cloverly Formation fauna in Wyoming and Montana.[68] The dinosaur faunas from these formations are significantly more diverse than the fauna known from Maryland and Virginia, but this is likely due to the fact that the fauna here is not well sampled due to limited outcrops. [83] This suggests that the Patuxent and Arundel dinosaur faunas of our region may yet be significantly expanded through future collecting. Another point to take away from these comparisons is that, in the early Albian stage of the Early Cretaceous, the dinosaur fauna across the entire continent of North America was quite similar and represented a single, continent-wide assemblage of animals that did not vary significantly from east to west, though it did vary perceptibly from south to north.

CHAPTER

9

LATE CRETACEOUS, CENOMANIAN:

THE BEGINNING OF APPALACHIA

The exposed Mesozoic stratigraphic record in Virginia ends with the upper Lower to lowermost Upper Cretaceous Patapsco Formation. During the Late Cretaceous, the western Virginia Coastal Plain region was gently warped upward into an east-west trending arch that shed sediment north, east, and south away from the western Virginia Coastal Plain. This arching was slight, but it was enough to prevent sediment from being preserved in this area. Throughout the western coastal plain of Virginia, the Lower Cretaceous Patuxent and Patapsco formations are directly overlain by the Lower Paleogene (Paleocene) Aquia Formation.[84] A deeply buried record of Upper Cretaceous strata exists in the eastern Coastal Plain of Virginia, but it is only accessible through deep drilling and coring. Fortunately, sediments deposited during this time interval are accessible both to the north of Virginia in Maryland, Delaware, and southern New Jersey, and to the south in North and South Carolina. A summary of these units and their ages is shown in Figure 25.

Soon after the deposition of the Lower Cretaceous Patuxent and Arundel formations, major tectonic changes in western North America caused the entire region known today as the Great Plains to sink beneath the ocean and form a mid-continent inland sea called the Western Interior Seaway (Figure 26). The spread of this seaway cut the eastern part of North America off from surrounding land masses to form a separate island-continent that has been named Appalachia.[85] Because the animals and plants that lived on the island-continent of Appalachia became isolated from animals and plants that lived in western North America in a land called Laramidia, they began to evolve into new and unique forms different from those then living in western North America and the rest of the Late Cretaceous world. This contrast in the vertebrate faunas of the two regions later became even more pronounced because, during

PERIOD	EPOCH	AGE	Ma	Land Vertebrate Faunal Stages	NORTH CAROLINA	MARYLAND/ DELAWARE	NEW JERSEY
CRETACEOUS	LATE	MAASTRICHTIAN	66	Lancian	Peedee Formation	Severn Formation	New Egypt Fm. / Tinton Fm.
							Red Bank Fm.
			72	Edmontian			Navesink Fm.
		CAMPANIAN		Kirtlandian	Donoho Creek Formation	Mount Laurel Sand	Mount Laurel Sand
					Bladen Fm.		Wenonah Fm.
							Marshalltown Fm.
				Judithian	Coachman Fm.	Englishtown Fm.	Englishtown Fm.
					Cane Acre Fm.		Woodbury Fm.
			84		Caddin Fm.	Merchantville Fm.	Merchantville Fm.
		SANTONIAN			Shepherd Grove Fm.		
			86		Cape Fear Fm. / Pleasant Creek Fm.	Magothy Formation	Magothy Formation
		CONIACIAN	90	not yet named			
		TURONIAN	94				
		CENOMANIAN			Clubhouse Formation	Raritan Formation	Raritan Formation
			100			Patapsco Fm., Elk Neck beds	

Figure 25 – *Summary diagram of the Late Cretaceous stratigraphic units found in the coastal plains of New Jersey, Delaware, Maryland, and North Carolina.*[86] *Source for figure shown in Appendix 2.*

much of the Late Cretaceous, Laramidia in western North America was connected to Asia across Alaska and Siberia. This connection allowed a considerable number of Asian dinosaur species to enter western North America and become established there, but these animals were unable to move eastward because the Western Interior Seaway blocked them from Appalachia.

By the beginning of the Late Cretaceous, a transformation known as the Cretaceous Terrestrial Revolution had occurred in which flowering plants rapidly came to dominate the fields and understory forests of

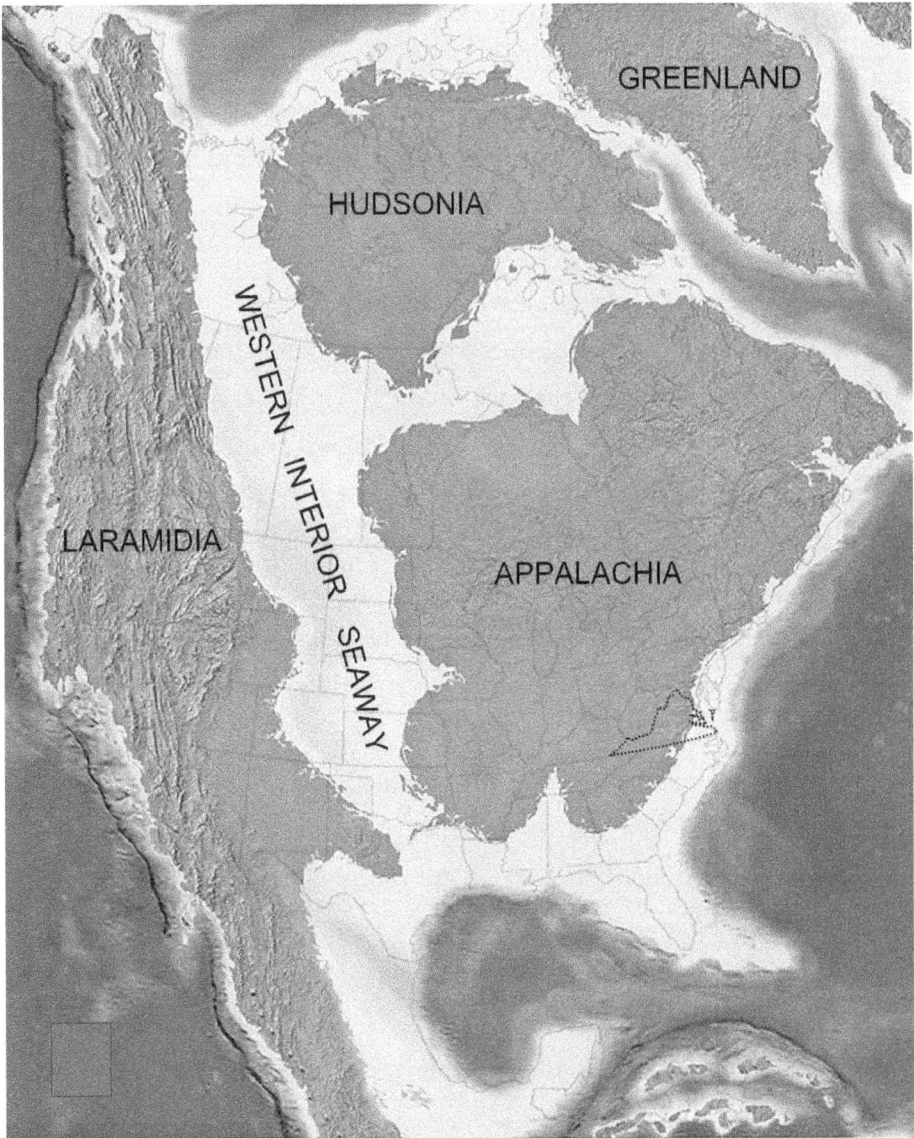

Figure 26 – The paleogeography of North America during the Campanian stage of the Creta-ceous. Location of Virginia indicated by dashed outline. Source for figure shown in Appendix 2.

the Earth. Appalachia was a part of this transformation, as evidenced by the Cenomanian flora of the Virginia region, best known from New Jersey. Unlike the earlier Patuxent flora, of which about 6% were flow-ering plants, and the Patapsco flora, of which about 22% were flowering plants, nearly 60% of the Cenomanian flora consisted of a very diverse array of flowering plants that dominated the meadow and understory vegetational environments. The ascendance of flowering plants at the beginning of the Late Cretaceous in the Virginia region was accompanied by the disappearance of a great many ferns, tree ferns, and plants from an extinct group called cycadeoids that all had been common in Patuxent time.

Other trees, such as auracarians, redwoods, cycads, and gingkos, persisted in the Virginia region during the Cenomanian, though they do not exist naturally in the area today.[87] Unlike earlier in the Cretaceous, a modern visitor to the Cenomanian landscape would find many familiar trees and shrubs closely related to living Virginia trees and shrubs, such as maple, fig, holly, walnut, laurel, magnolia, bayberry, plane tree, oak, willow, sassafras, and viburnum. Today, these floral components are typically found in well-watered and forested landscapes, and the same was probably true then. Based on the known paleolatitude of the Virginia region, the climate would have been transitional between subtropical and warm temperate. This conclusion is supported by the fact that close modern relatives of the component plants of the Cenomanian flora all are found commonly today within this latitudinal belt.

Although a number of Late Cretaceous formations are exposed in the New Jersey to North Carolina region, dinosaur and other vertebrate remains are known only from a few of them, and these are mostly of Campanian and Maastrichtian age. In the earlier part of the Late Cretaceous, dinosaur and other vertebrate remains are very scarce and known from only three sites in two Cenomanian formations. The most significant site among these is a recently described footprint locality at the NASA Goddard Space Flight Center in Maryland.[88] This locality adds significant new information about the earliest Late Cretaceous dinosaurs and other contemporaneous animals that lived in the Maryland region, including Virginia (Table 1). This ichnofauna

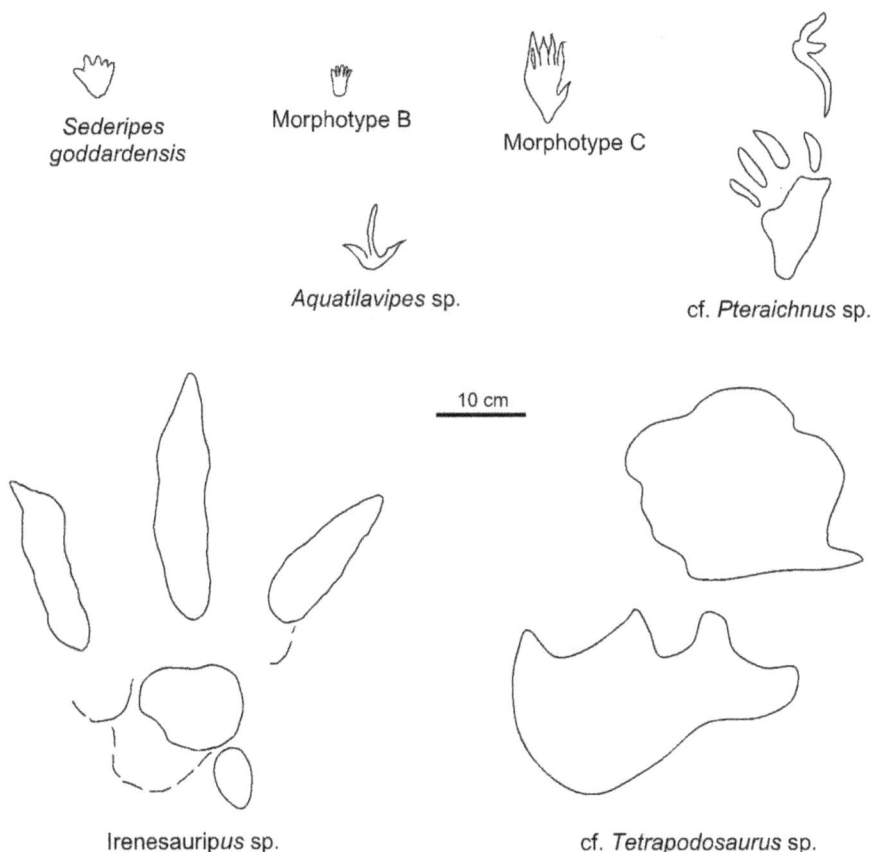

Figure 27 – Types of fossil footprints known from Cenomanian strata in Maryland and New Jersey. Sederipes and "morphotypes B and C" are mammal tracks, Pteraichnus is a pterosaur track, Aquatilavipes is likely a bird track, Irenesauripus is a theropod dinosaur track, and Tetrapodosaurus is an ankylosaur track. Sources for figure shown in Appendix 2.

(Figure 27) includes tracks of a pterosaur (cf. *Pteraichnus* sp.), a bird (*Aquatilavipes* sp.), an ankylosaur (cf. *Tetrapodosaurus*), and three kinds of small mammals.[89] One mammal track was named from this site (*Sederipes goddardensis*), but tracks of two others kinds of mammals can neither be referred to any existing ichnotaxon, nor are they well enough preserved to be named. The exceptional number of tracks referable to small animals at the Goddard site could indicate that the abundant mammal tracks represent an exceptionally mammal-friendly environment throughout all of Appalachia. However, it is equally plausible to argue, based on the very few faunal sites so far known in this region, that there was simply a favorable local environment at the Goddard site that was not typical of most other regions of Appalachia.

The other two Cenomanian localities are in New Jersey. A site near Roebling yielded a carnosaur metatarsal of somewhat uncertain stratigraphic provenance that could have come from either the late Cenomanian Raritan Formation or the Santonian Magothy Formation. [90] The other New Jersey site, located near Woodbridge, yielded a carnosaur trackway referable to the ichnogenus *Irenesauripus* that was found in the Woodbridge Member of the late Cenomanian Raritan Formation. The two New Jersey localities demonstrate that relatively large carnivores continued to hunt prey in Appalachia even after it became a separate small continent.

The sparse Cenomanian vertebrate fauna so far known from eastern Appalachia shows a general continuity with the earlier faunas found in the Patuxent and Arundel formations. Even though many Patuxent/Arundel taxa have not been found yet in Cenomanian strata, forms that are obviously derived from Patuxent/Arundel ancestors show up in the next younger known Campanian deposits. This strongly suggests that intermediate animals persisted through the Cenomanian along the eastern border of Appalachia that simply have not been found so far. Two exceptions to this pattern are the apparent loss of both iguanodontid dinosaurs and the very large sauropod dinosaur *Astrodon johnstoni*, neither of which is known from any Late Cretaceous stratigraphic intervals in the Virginia region. With these exceptions, even as Appalachia became isolated from Laramidia, it seems to have continued to support a fauna grossly similar to that which had been present in the region toward the end of the Early Cretaceous.

CHAPTER

10

LATE CRETACEOUS, CAMPANIAN:

LATER LIFE ON THE CONTINENT OF APPALACHIA

Only during the last two stages of the Cretaceous, the Campanian and Maastrichtian, are abundantly fossiliferous strata found in the Virginia region that produce significant numbers of dinosaur and other vertebrate remains. These fossiliferous strata and their relative ages are summarized in Figure 25. Most of the Campanian strata in this region formed in shallow marine environments that were close enough to shore to occasionally collect remains of dinosaurs that washed out to sea during floods or drifted out to sea as bloated carcasses.

Unlike in the older Mesozoic terrestrial strata exposed in Virginia and nearby states, the Campanian and Maastrichtian Upper Cretaceous deposits in the Atlantic Coastal Plain also include an abundant and diverse marine vertebrate fauna. Among this marine fauna, remains of bony fishes are not well collected or studied. Even so, 16 genera are known (Table 1, some shown in Figure 28) including the peculiar and specialized bony fish genera *Anomoeodus, Enchodus,* and *Xiphactinus*.[91] The only genus among these fish that still persists in today's oceans is the ladyfish, *Albula*. Another very interesting member of this marine fish fauna was the lobe-finned coelacanth fish *Megalocoelacanthus*, which was about ten feet in length. It was closely related to the "living fossil" coelacanth fish *Latimeria*, which still lives today in deep waters of the Indian Ocean. *Megalocoelacanthus* was the last coelacanth fish known to have lived in the North American region before its entire lineage died out forever in this part of the world.

Twenty-four genera of sharks and 15 genera of rays are known from the Campanian marine beds.[92] Many of these disappeared in the end-Cretaceous extinction event that was later to come, but some represent forms that would survive to become the ancestors of a number of genera of sharks and rays living today. Among the sharks, Cretaceous genera still living today include the sand tiger shark *Carcharias*, the sand shark *Odontaspis*, the dogfish shark *Squalus*, and the angel shark *Squatina*. Among the rays, Cretaceous genera still living today include the stingray *Dasyatis*, the eagle ray *Myliobatis*, and the skate *Raja*.

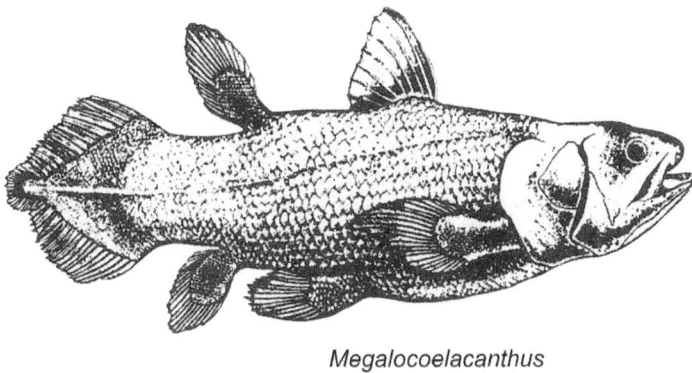

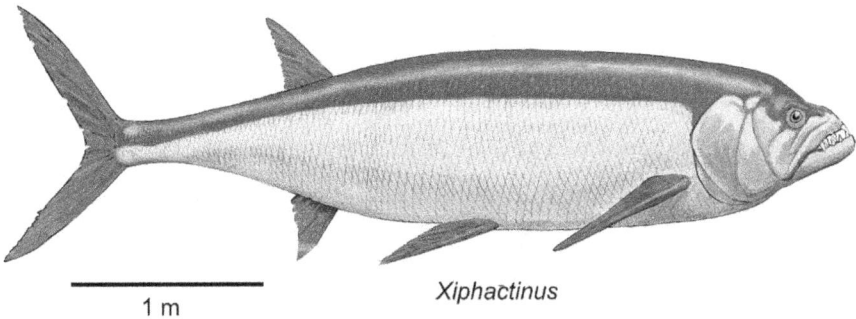

Albula

Anomoeodus

Enchodus

Megalocoelacanthus

1 m

Xiphactinus

Figure 28 – Marine fishes known from the Campanian stage in the Virginia region. Sources for figure shown in Appendix 2.

Marine reptiles also were abundant in these waters (Figure 29). A primitive hard-shelled sea turtle called *Euclastes* was present, along with two early representatives of the leatherback sea turtle lineage, *Atlantochelys* and *Corsochelys*.[93] Remains of a Campanian long-necked plesiosaur that can only be identified as belonging to the family Elasmosauridae have been found in North Carolina. It may belong to the genus *Cimoliasaurus*, which is known from diagnostic material found in the slightly younger Maastrichtian beds of the Atlantic Coastal Plain.[94]

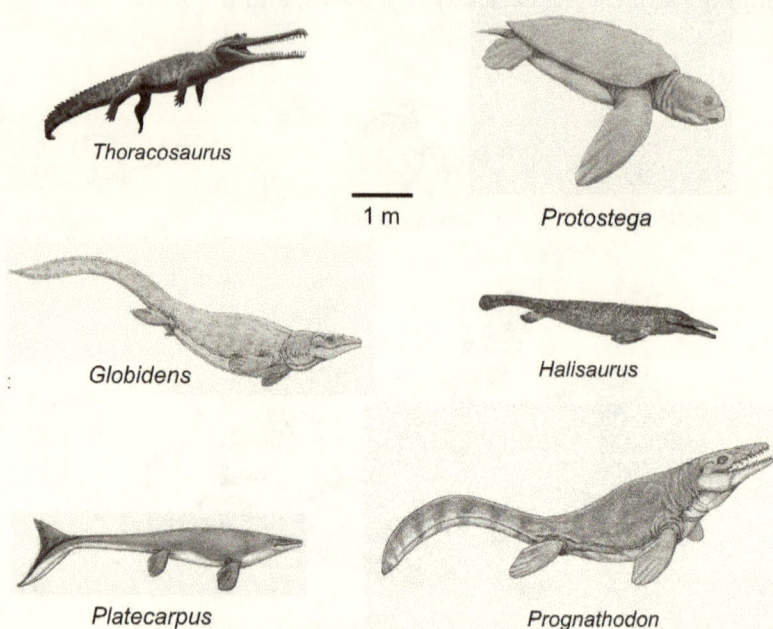

Figure 29 – Marine reptiles known from the Campanian stage in the Virginia region.
Sources for figure shown in Appendix 2.

Most abundant and diverse at that time were a group of marine reptiles called mosasaurs. These gigantic marine-going lizards had come to dominate the top predator roles in the seas during the latter part of the Late Cretaceous.[95] Six kinds of these animals have been reported from the Campanian deposits along the Atlantic Coast. None can be identified to a particular species, but they can be assigned to the genera *Clidastes, Globidens, Halisaurus, Platecarpus, Prognathodon*, and *Tylosaurus*. One kind of sea-going crocodilian, *Thoracosaurus neocessariensis*, also was an inhabitant of this realm.[96] It apparently was almost completely adapted to life in the seas, for its remains have never been reported from Campanian freshwater deposits.

Notably missing in this list are ichthyosaurs. These very dolphin-like marine reptiles had appeared in the Triassic Period and were very abundant throughout the Jurassic (see *Ophthalmosaurus*, Figure 19), but then began to dwindle in numbers through the Early Cretaceous. They were extinct by the Late Cretaceous, becoming one of the few major groups of Mesozoic reptiles that died out well before the end of the Mesozoic.[97]

By the Campanian, the southeastern United States was everywhere rich in flowering plants except for its forest canopies, which continued to be dominated by several kinds of coniferous trees, including trees ancestral to Norfolk Island pines, bald cypresses, and redwoods. The rise of a vegetational landscape dominated by flowering plants opened up a host of opportunities for insects, many of which quickly evolved to take advantage of nectar and fruit being produced by these rapidly diversifying flowering plants. Similar opportunities also appeared for adaptable groups of herbivores such as the ornithischian dinosaurs. This profound change in the food resources of this region was likely the most important reason why the Late Cretaceous dinosaur faunas in North America became so different from the dinosaur faunas that had existed during the earlier Mesozoic.

The dinosaur fauna of Appalachia had diverged markedly by the Campanian from the dinosaur fauna of Laramidia. Unfortunately, no abundant dinosaur fossils have been found anywhere in Appalachia. What we have found so far consists mostly of rare and fragmentary specimens found in Campanian units that accumulated in marine waters. Fortunately, a few nearshore and even inshore Campanian deposits are preserved, and these have yielded most of the better Late Cretaceous dinosaur remains found so far along the coastal borders of Appalachia.[83]

One of the most striking things about the dinosaur fauna of Appalachia is the complete absence of sauropods. During the Campanian, the western world of Laramidia also lacked sauropods, so sauropods went extinct not only in Appalachia, but also throughout all of North America during most of the Late Cretaceous. It may be that the splitting of the

Early Cretaceous continent of North America into the three smaller land bodies of Appalachia, Hudsonia, and Laramidia (Figure 26) did not provide sauropods with enough room to maintain successful populations in any of the remaining smaller land areas. Late in the Maastrichtian stage, just before the dinosaurs went extinct globally, the sauropod genus *Alamosaurus* appeared in Laramidia. It apparently migrated back into that region from Asia, or by island-hopping from South America, which then was separated by oceanic waters from North America. In either case, as far as we know, *Alamosaurus* failed to reach Appalachia. By the beginning of the Late Cretaceous, the sauropods were apparently gone from Appalachia and were never to return.

Similarly, advanced ceratopsian families evolved from the earlier and more primitive neoceratopsian group after Appalachia became isolated from Laramidia, so these advanced groups never had an opportunity to become established in Appalachia during the Campanian. The same was true for the crested hadrosaur group, as well as several groups of smaller dinosaurs abundant in Laramidia during the Campanian, such as the ankylosaurs, troodontids, pachycephalosaurs, and caenagnathids.

The most abundant Campanian dinosaur remains found in Appalachia are those of flat-headed hadrosaurs,[98] popularly known as duck-billed dinosaurs. At least four types are known. The smallest is called *"Hadrosaurus" minor* (Table 1). The generic name is used in quotation marks because, although it was originally described under the genus name *Hadrosaurus*, recent work indicates that it does not belong in that genus. So far, no more appropriate name has been proposed, so the name *Hadrosaurus* continues to be used but in quotation marks. The second type is another small hadrosaurid named *Lophorhothon*, which has been found in Alabama and North Carolina. Remains of a third, somewhat larger type, a true *Hadrosaurus*, have been found in the Atlantic Coastal Plain in New Jersey, Maryland, North Carolina, and South Carolina (Figure 30). This dinosaur, named *Hadrosaurus foulkii*, is notable because

Appalachiosaurus

Dryptosaurus

Lophorhothon

1 m

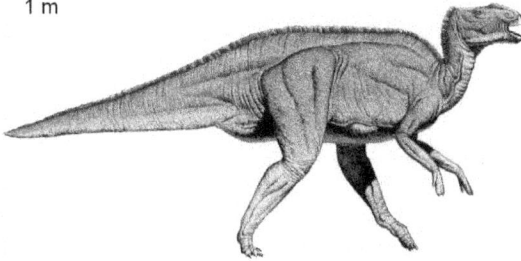

Hadrosaurus

Figure 30 – Large dinosaurs known from the Campanian stage in the Virginia region.
Sources for figure shown in Appendix 2.

it was the first fairly complete dinosaur skeletal species described from anywhere in the world. A much larger fourth hadrosaur, *Hypsibema*, is known from Missouri, North Carolina, and New Jersey. *Hypsibema* was by far the largest herbivore to roam Appalachia and may have been up to sixty feet in length. Like other ornithopods, it was probably a herding animal that occupied the ecological niche that sauropods once had held in the days before Appalachia became an island continent.

Besides hadrosaurs, two other kinds of herbivorous dinosaur are known from Appalachia. One, recently documented from a jaw fragment found in North Carolina, was a leptoceratopsid ceratopsian (*Montanoceratops*, Figure 31). This family includes rather primitive, diminutive, and hornless relatives of the much larger, horned ceratopsians of Laramidia and Asia. Also present in New Jersey are remains of a nodosaurid armored herbivore. Only isolated pieces of its armor have been found, so identification so far can be made only to the family level. This animal was similar in appearance to the much better-known nodosaurid *Panoplosaurus*.

The most diverse group of dinosaurs recovered from the fringes of Appalachia are the theropods. A number of carnivorous theropod genera have been identified, including the largest and probably top predator in the region, *Appalachiosaurus montgomeriensis*. It was a very large tyrannosaurid, though not quite as large as its famous cousin *Tyrannosaurus rex*. The only well-preserved skeleton of *Appalachiosaurus* found so far belongs to a subadult animal that was about 25 feet in length, so an adult probably would have been in the size range of 35 feet or more.

A somewhat smaller but still quite formidable carnivore was *Dryptosaurus*, which is estimated to have reached an adult length of about 25 feet. Among carnivores in the smaller size-ranges was *Saurornitholestes*. It was about six feet long and weighed only about twenty pounds. It was a rather bird-like dromaeosaur related to *Velociraptor*, with sharp, sickle-shaped claws on its feet. Like *Deinonychus* in the Early Cretaceous, *Saurornitholestes* likely hunted in groups. A fourth kind of theropod, probably not adapted to a strictly carnivorous lifestyle, was an ostrich-mimic dinosaur, "*Ornithomimus*," which belongs to the family Ornithomimidae. The correct generic placement of this species is debated, so for now it is placed in quotation marks until a proper generic

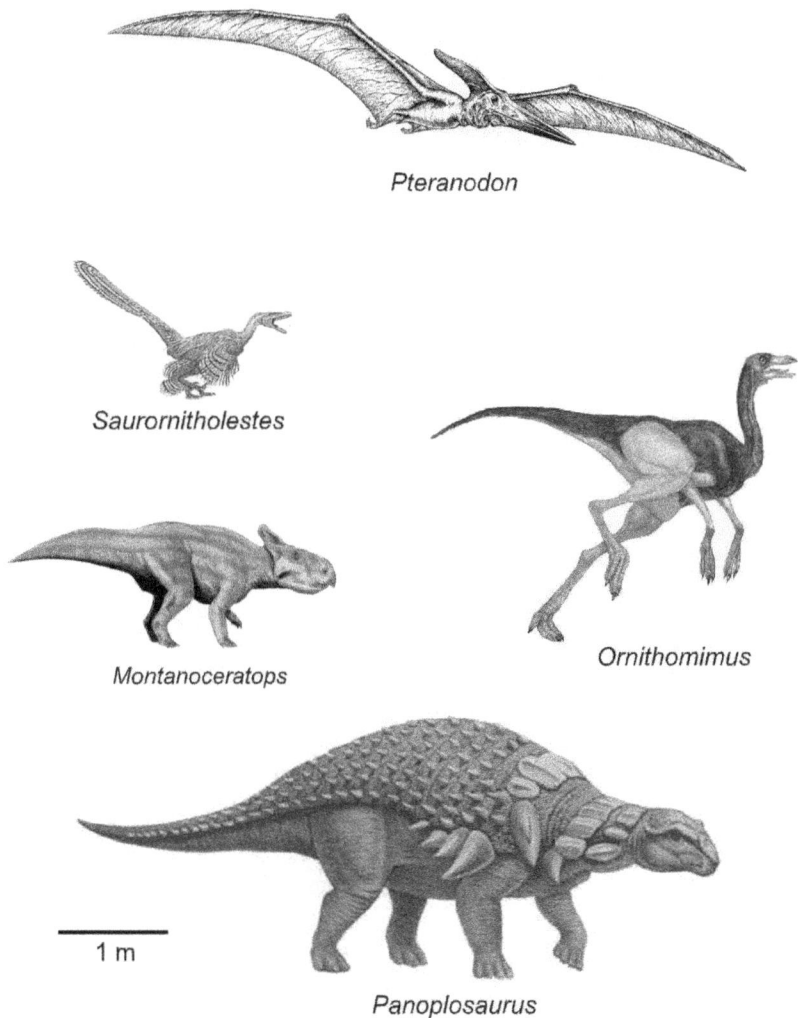

Figure 31 – Smaller dinosaurs and a pterosaur (Pteranodon) known from the Campanian stage in the Virginia region. Sources for figure shown in Appendix 2.

name can be established. This animal, as its family name suggests, was probably rather like an ostrich and ran in fleet-footed herds.

Underfoot of the dinosaurs of Appalachia were a variety of lizards (Figure 32). At least eight different types of Campanian terrestrial lizards have been identified in New Jersey.[99] Their remains are mostly fragmentary but can still be identified as belonging to the living families Helodermatidae, Iguanidae, Necrosauridae, Xenosauridae, and Anguidae. *Haptosphenus*, a lizard belonging to the extinct family Chamopsiidae, and

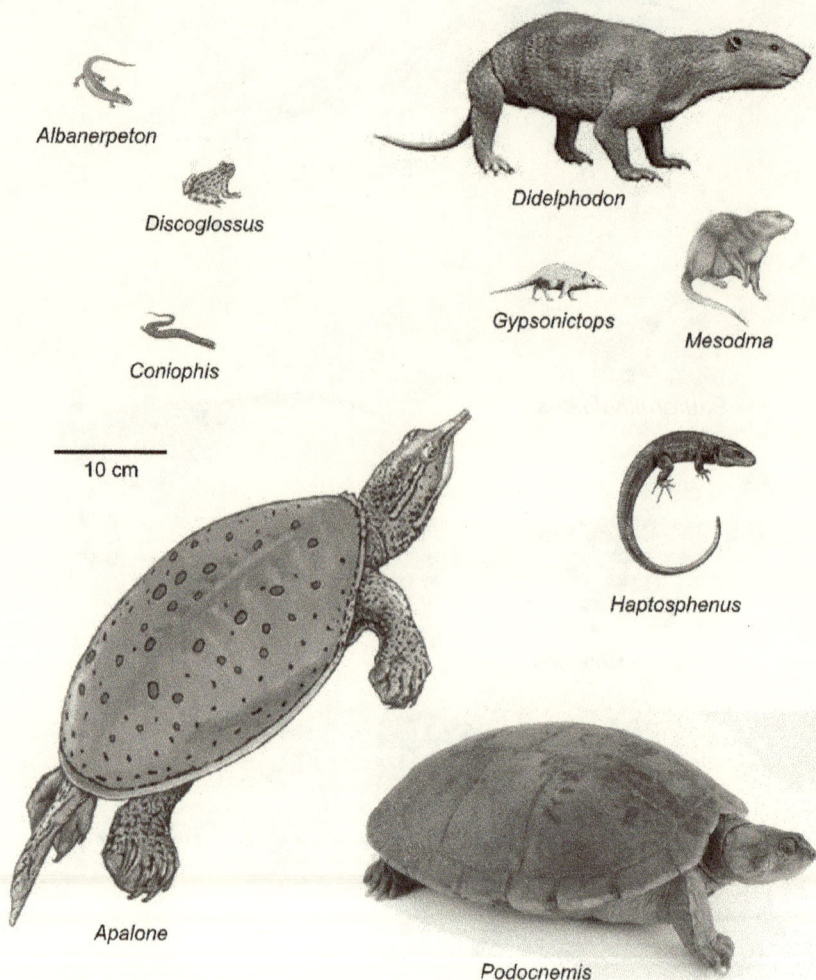

Figure 32 – Small amphibians (Albanerpeton, Discoglossus), soft-shell turtle (Apalone), side-necked turtle (Podocnemis), lizard (Haptosphenus), snake (Coniophis), and mammals (Didelphodon, Mesodma, Gypsonictops) known from the Campanian stage in the Virginia region. Sources for figure shown in Appendix 2.

Prototeius, which belongs to the living family Teiidae, are the only lizards identified to a generic or species level. While the record of lizards in Appalachia remains sparse and poorly known, it is good enough to indicate that lizards were both abundant and diverse here during the Campanian.

Six kinds of small mammals have been recovered in Appalachia from New Jersey and North Carolina.[100] Four are rather rodent-like animals called multituberculates, which either burrowed or lived in trees. Even though these animals lived a rodent-like lifestyle, they were not very closely related to any living mammal group. They are the only major branch of true mammals to have become completely extinct. Although multituberculates are not well known or well publicized, they have at least a hundred-million-year fossil history, which is the longest of any mammalian lineage. Two of these small multituberculates can only be identified as belonging to the families Cimolomyidae and Cimolodontidae, but the other two have been tentatively identified as *Cimolodon* and *Mesodma*. Two more mammalian groups are also present. One, a carnivore, belongs to the family Stagodontidae (*Didelphodon* is a close relative). This animal was distantly related to modern marsupials. The other can be identified as a eutherian mammal (similar to *Gypsonictops*), which is the group of mammals to which we and most of the common mammals of today belong.

Based on what we know from elsewhere in the world, birds were probably abundant in the trees and skies of Appalachia during the Late Cretaceous. So far, however, nothing has been found to demonstrate this. What can be documented, however, are pterosaurs. In Delaware, pterosaur remains have been found that are assigned to *Pteranodon* or a closely related form. *Pteranodon* had an estimated wingspan of 19 feet and looked similar to a modern albatross. This has led to the suggestion that *Pteranodon* was likely a high seas glider, cruising above the surface of the Late Cretaceous western Atlantic Ocean looking for fish. Another pterosaur that may have been present in the Virginia region was the very large azhdarchid *Arambourgiania philadelphiae*, with an estimated wingspan of around 35 feet. This animal has been found in Campanian beds in western Tennessee, so in all likelihood it was present in Virginia as well.[101] The flight capabilities of these pterosaurs suggest that they could easily have crossed the Western Interior Seaway back and forth between Appalachia and Laramidia, so they probably did not belong to species that were indigenous to Appalachia.

These varied dinosaurs and pterosaurs lived in Appalachia along with a variety of crocodilians.[102] Even as early as the Late Cretaceous, most crocodilians could be placed into one of the three living crocodilian groups: alligators-caimans, crocodiles, and gavials-gharials (which are now confined to southern Asia). Three genera were abundant in Appalachia, two of which belonged to the alligator-caiman group. The largest of these was *Deinosuchus* (Figure 33), which ranged up to 35 feet in length and weighed around ten tons (twenty thousand pounds). Stomach remains found with skeletons of this animal indicate that its diet mostly consisted of turtles and fish, but it seems obvious that any dinosaur living in Appalachia also would be fair game if it was foolish enough to get too close to the waters where this very large ambush predator was lurking. The other alligatorine type was *Brachychampsa*, which was considerably smaller and ranged only up to about ten feet in length. The third type of crocodilian was *Borealosuchus*, which belonged to the gavial-gharial group and ranged up to about nine feet in length. These three genera of crocodilians also occurred in Laramidia during the Campanian, but at the species level, they are all different from the western species. This provides strong evidence that these three animals all were endemic to Appalachia.

Brachychampsa

1 m

Borealosuchus

Deinosuchus

Figure 33 – Crocodilians known from the Campanian stage in the Virginia region. Sources for figure shown in Appendix 2.

Sharing the rivers and swamps of Appalachia with the crocodilians were a variety of turtles, salamanders, and frogs (Figure 32). Two types of primitive soft-shell turtles are commonly found that are called "*Trionyx*." Although they are distinctly different from each other and definitely members of the soft-shell turtle group, their proper generic name remains uncertain. They were described long ago under the name *Trionyx*, but in the latter part of the twentieth century, it was determined that this name can only be properly applied to certain Asian soft-shell species and not to any American forms. These Appalachian turtles are therefore not species of *Trionyx*, but until good skull material is found for at least one of them, they cannot be referred with confidence to any known fossil or living soft-shell turtle genus or be described as something new. Until then, we continue to call them "*Trionyx*" in quotation marks.

These soft-shelled turtles coexisted in the rivers and swamps of Appalachia with three kinds of large side-necked turtles called *Bothremys*, *Chedighaii*, and *Taphrosphys*. Their closest living relatives are found in South America, but in the Cretaceous, this family of turtles was common and widespread in southern North America. A sixth type of riverine turtle, *Adocus*, was distantly related to living American pond turtles. Although pond turtles today are widespread and very common in the southeastern United States, during the days of Appalachia, *Adocus* represented a new and minor component of its turtle fauna.[103]

Remains of both amphibians and frogs have been found in Appalachia.[104] Salamanders are represented by an indeterminate species of *Albanerpeton* in North Carolina, and the Ellisdale Fossil Site in New Jersey has yielded three kinds of salamander remains referable to *Parrisia*, to *Habrosaurus* or a closely related form, and to an indeterminate species within the family Sirenidae. So far, frogs are only known from New Jersey, where an indeterminate member of the family Hylidae lived along with other frogs closely related to the extinct genus *Eopelobates* and the living genus *Discoglossus*. These animals were not greatly different from salamanders and frogs living today, so in all likelihood they had very similar lifestyles.

The one freshwater Campanian fish reported from North Carolina is represented by isolated teeth attributed to the gar *Lepisosteus*. In New Jersey, remains have been recovered of a somewhat more diverse freshwater fish fauna (Table 1) that includes sturgeon (*Acipenser*), bowfin (*Amia*), and another type of gar (*Atractosteus*).[105]

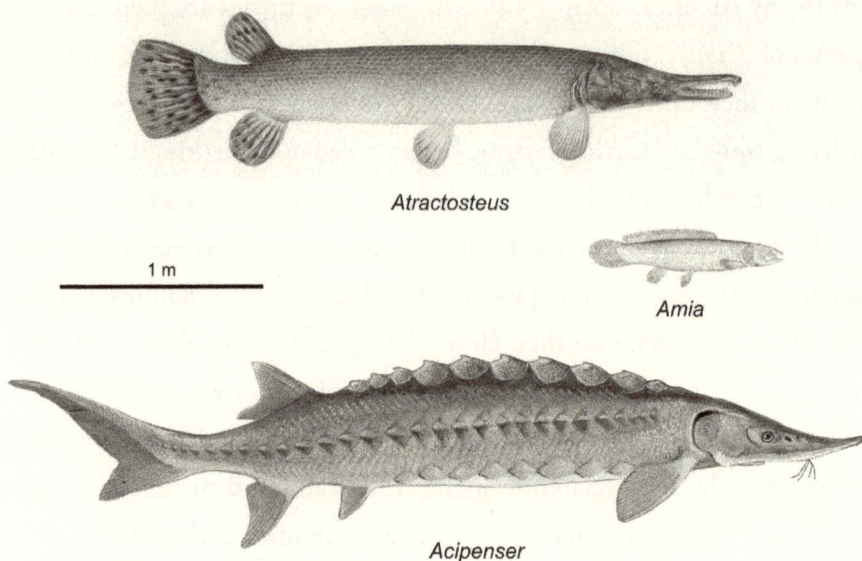

Atractosteus

1 m

Amia

Acipenser

Figure 34 – Freshwater fishes known from the Campanian stage in the Virginia region. Sources for figure shown in Appendix 2.

Because Appalachia was a small continent and isolated from the rest of the Campanian world, its dinosaurs were less diverse and on average smaller than the dinosaurs found elsewhere. In most other parts of the Campanian world, dinosaurs continued to diversify and on average grow ever larger.[106] In the southern continents of Australia, South America, and Africa plus India (which then was still attached to Africa), dinosaur faunas had also changed greatly from the Early Cretaceous, but in ways quite different from the dinosaur faunas found in the more northerly continents. Huge sauropods called titanosaurs continued to be abundant and diverse there. Ornithischian dinosaurs were often absent or else a minor component of the fauna. Predator roles were filled by peculiar carnivores called abelisaurs and spinosaurs, along with very large carcharo-dontosaurs, which were by then extinct in North America. In Laramidia, Europe, and Asia (except India), dinosaur populations also had changed greatly from the Early Cretaceous, but in very different ways from the southern continents. Within this more northerly realm, horned ceratop-sians, crested hadrosaurs, and feathered maniraptoran theropods greatly diversified, increased in size, and dominated the landscapes. Europe was somewhat of a mixed bag, having many dinosaurs similar to those else-where in the northern continents, but at the same time harboring among them a scattering of species more typical of Africa. The transformation of the dinosaur world in the northern continents occurred while flowering plants were diversifying and spreading across the world, so it seems likely that these two events were closely interconnected.

Oceanic life offshore from Virginia was abundant and diverse, and it had no obvious barriers to migration into or out of the waters around Appalachia. Even so, the marine reptiles along the eastern coast of Ap-palachia are not known to have been as diverse as those found offshore of the western border of Appalachia. The western border of Appalachia was adjacent to the Western Interior Seaway, which was a very broad and relatively shallow sea that was somewhat protected from large storms both on its east and on its west. In contrast, the eastern coast of Ap-palachia was probably subject to large oceanic storms that, like today, caused widespread coastal damage to the breeding and nesting habitats of animals that lived there. Even so, despite the inherent dangers that come from being located on an oceanic coastline, life in and around Appalachia was abundant and diverse both on land and in the sea in Campanian time.

CHAPTER

11

LATE CRETACEOUS, MAASTRICHTIAN:

THE END OF THE MESOZOIC WORLD AND THE DAWN OF THE CENOZOIC ERA

In the eastern United States, sea levels were generally much higher in the early Maastrichtian than they had been in the Campanian. As in the Campanian, Maastrichtian beds are deeply buried in Virginia, but they are exposed both to its north and south. In North Carolina, the Maastrichtian is represented by a unit called the Peedee Formation, which is essentially age-equivalent to beds in Maryland called the Severn Formation. In New Jersey, the Maastrichtian interval is divided into the Navesink Formation, the Red Bank Sand, and the Tinton Sand in ascending order (Figure 25). Most of the nearshore strata associated with this sea level rise were later removed by erosion, so what remains in most areas are offshore strata that preferentially preserve remains of Maastrichtian marine animals. The only Maastrichtian nearshore or inshore deposits found along the Eastern Seaboard are in New Jersey. In the late Maastrichtian, sea levels dropped substantially, quite possibly due to glaciers beginning to form in Antarctica. This sea level drop meant that no strata of this age are preserved above modern sea level anywhere in the Atlantic Coastal Plain. This late Maastrichtian sea level drop also seems to have substantially drained the Western Interior Seaway and created a land bridge between Laramidia and Appalachia (Figure 35).

The evidence for a land bridge across the Western Interior Seaway comes from two places. In New Jersey, remains of a late Maastrichtian lambeosaurine (crested) hadrosaur have been found.[107] This specimen is not identifiable to a particular genus or species, but it may well belong to the contemporaneous crested hadrosaur *Hypacrosaurus* (Figure 36), which is well-known from age-equivalent beds in Laramidia. The discovery of this animal demonstrates that crested hadrosaurs finally reached New Jersey from Laramidia late in the Maastrichtian.

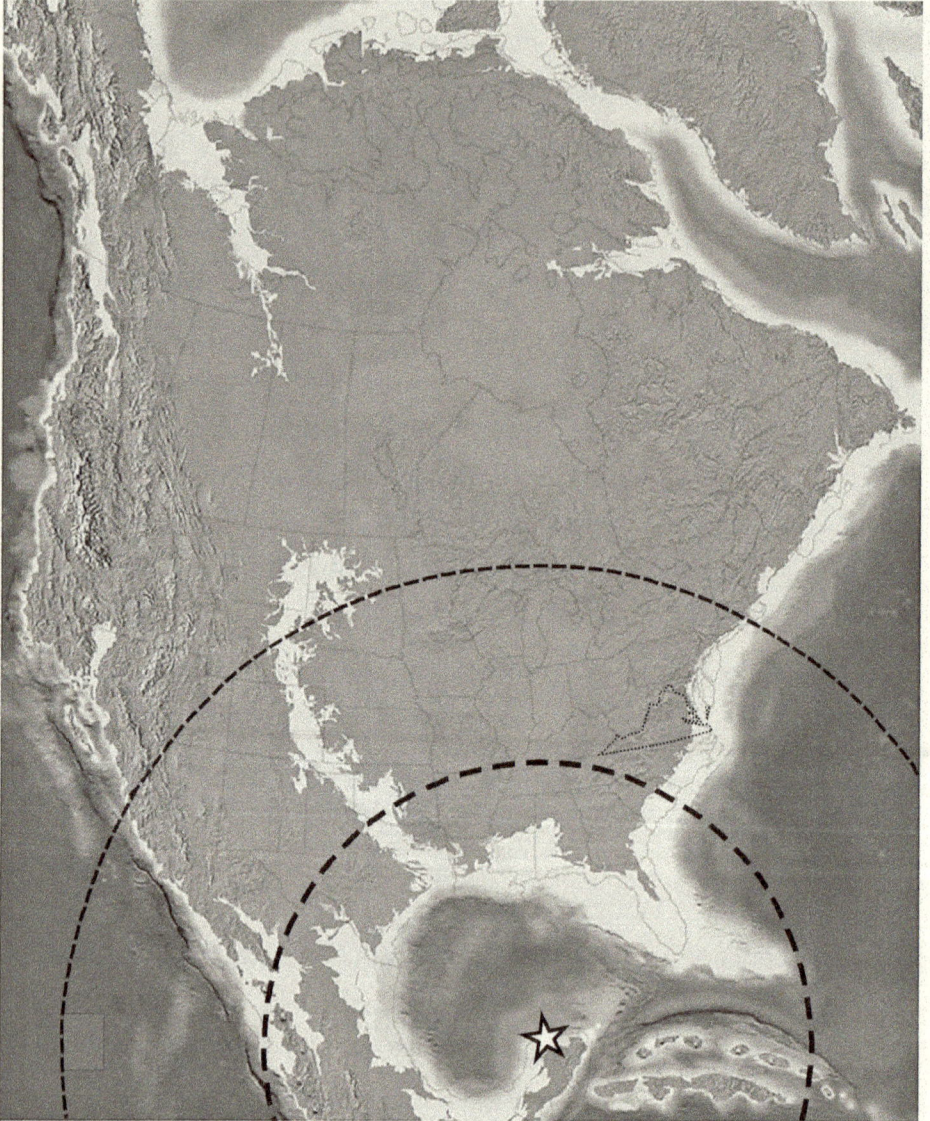

Figure 35 – The paleogeography of North America during the Maastrichtian stage of the Creta-ceous Location of Virginia indicated by dotted border; star locates impact site of the Chicxulub Crater in Mexico; dashed lines around impact site show (inner circle) the estimated limit of total forest flattening and (outer circle) limit of gale to hurricane force winds generated by this impact. Sources for figure shown in Appendix 2.

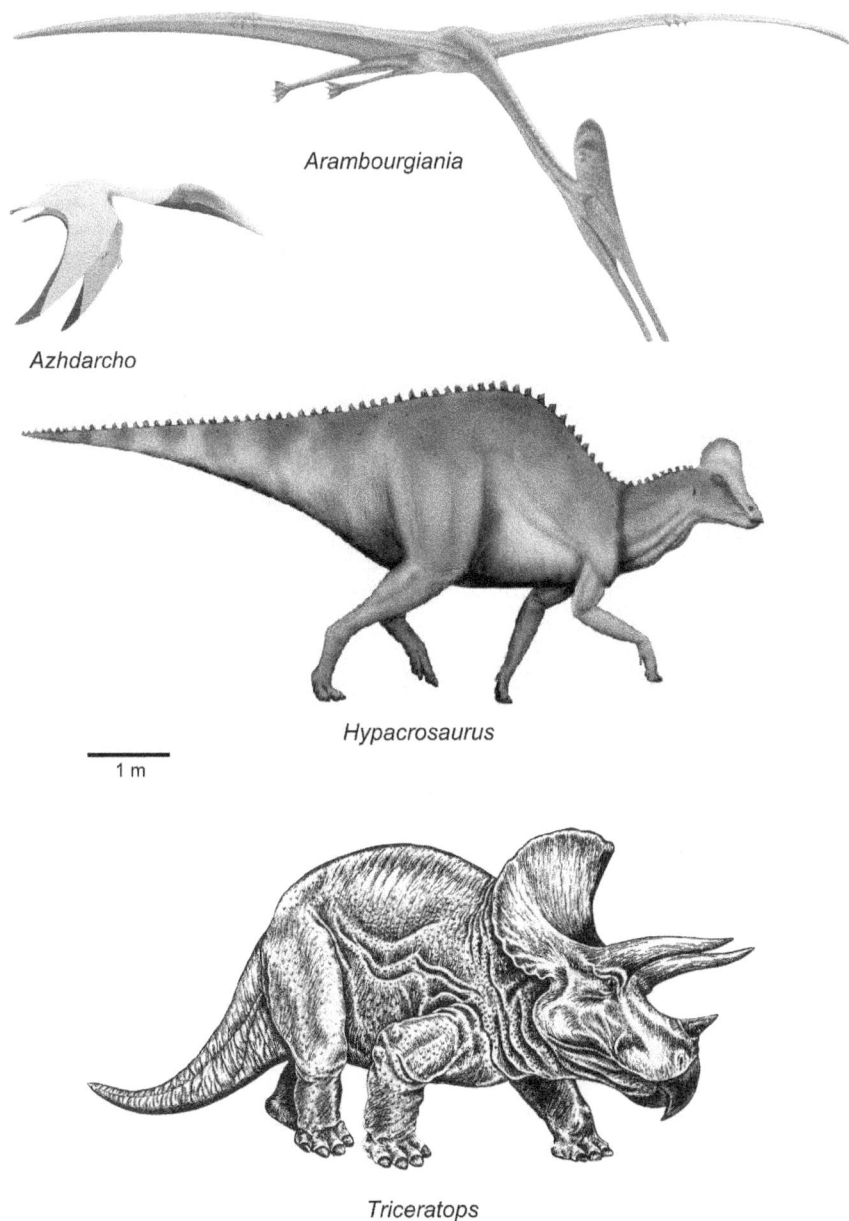

Figure 36 – Large pterosaurs and dinosaurs known from the Virginia region during the Maastrichtian stage of the Cretaceous. Sources for figure shown in Appendix 2.

There is no evidence from before this time that crested hadrosaurs were ever present in the small continent of Appalachia in eastern North America.

The second piece of evidence is the discovery of a tooth of a horned ceratopsian dinosaur in late Maastrichtian strata in northeastern Mississippi.[108] Based on the age of this discovery, it is likely that this tooth pertains to either *Torosaurus* or *Triceratops*, which were among the last of the late Maastrichtian Laramidian ceratopsians. This is the first evidence to show that this group of dinosaurs also managed to reach eastern North America in the late Maastrichtian, shortly before they became extinct with nearly all other dinosaurs at the very end of the Cretaceous. What these discoveries tell us is that in the later Maastrichtian, the dinosaur fauna of Appalachia finally was beginning to become infused with new dinosaurs that were arriving from Laramidia.

Despite the appearance of new arrivals, a number of Appalachia dinosaurs known from the Campanian persisted into the Maastrichtian. [109] These persistent endemics included the carnivore *Dryptosaurus*, a second, even larger carnivore likely descended from *Appalachiosaurus*, the ostrich-mimic dinosaur "*Ornithomimus*," and the two species of *Hadrosaurus*, *H. foulkii* and "*H.*" *minor*. In addition, one or more species of tank-like, herbivorous nodosaurids also continued to survive (Figure 31).

Remains of non-dinosaurian land animals are also sparse in the Maastrichtian strata of eastern North America. The only mammal so far reported from the Maastrichtian is a femur of an indeterminate multituberculate found in New Jersey.[110] Also from New Jersey have come remains of a very large pterosaur called *Arambourgiania philadelphiae*. This animal was closely related to *Quetzalcoatlus* and equally gigantic. *Arambourgiania* is estimated to have had a wingspan of about 35 feet and, when standing, may have been about 15 feet tall. Like other members of its pterosaurian group, it had unusually long legs and a long neck. Its appearance was somewhat stork-like, and this has led to the suggestion that it may have lived a similar lifestyle, often walking in shallow waters looking for fish to catch with its long beak. A relatively much smaller pterosaur has been described from North Carolina that probably had a wingspan of about 15 feet. It is also an azhdarchid pterosaur, but it belonged to a smaller genus, possibly *Azhdarcho*.[111] The only bird so far positively identified from the Maastrichtian beds of eastern North America is *Telmatornis* (Figure 37), which was a prehistoric shorebird.[112] It was related to living waterfowls, which belong to one of the few groups of birds that survived the end-Cretaceous extinction.[113]

Better represented in the Maastrichtian strata of the eastern United States are freshwater aquatic reptiles. Maastrichtian turtles[114] include *Adocus, Agomphus, Bothremys, Osteopygis, Taphrosphys*, and two species of "*Trionyx*." *Agomphus* had a highly arched shell, suggesting that it may have lived a lifestyle similar to that of modern tortoises and box turtles. Among freshwater crocodylians, alligatorines were represented by *Deinosuchus*, which had persisted from the Campanian, and *Allognathosuchus* (Figure 37), which was new to this region. The appearance of another new genus, *Bottosaurus*, marks the earliest occurrence of the true crocodylian lineage in eastern North America.[115]

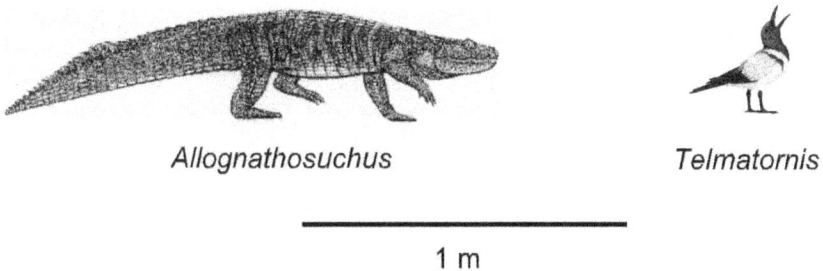

Allognathosuchus   *Telmatornis*

1 m

Figure 37 – An alligatorid crocodilian and a shore bird known from the Virginia region during the Maastrichtian stage of the Cretaceous. Sources for figure shown in Appendix 2.

Amphibian remains are completely unknown, but remains of a freshwater gar of indeterminate genus have been found.[116] Descendants of several other genera of freshwater fishes reported from the Campanian in Appalachia (*Acipenser, Amia, Atractosteus*) still exist in the southeastern United States, so it seems likely that they continued to exist here in Maastrichtian times even though their remains so far have not been discovered.

Of particular interest is the discovery of tooth plates of the lungfish *Ceratodus* in New Jersey (Figure 21). *Ceratodus* died out in Laramidia by the end of the Early Cretaceous, so its persistence in Appalachia throughout the Late Cretaceous makes it the last lungfish known to have lived anywhere in North America during the Late Cretaceous. Lungfish today are restricted to South America, Africa, and Australia, but in the Mesozoic, they were widely distributed around the globe.[117] Why they died out in the northern continents but survived in the southern ones remains a mystery. Probably the late survival of *Ceratodus* in Appalachia is at least in part due to its presence on an island continent insulated from changes that were taking place elsewhere in the northern hemisphere during the Late Cretaceous.

In the marine realm, little changed from the Campanian to the Maastrichtian. The marine fish fauna continued to be abundant and diverse. [118] Shark species had become more diverse, and ray species had become somewhat less diverse, but on average the overall abundance of the cartilaginous fishes was about the same as it had been in the Campanian. Similarly, an abundance of bony fish species have been reported.[119] One new bony fish appearance in the Maastrichtian western Atlantic was an extinct member of the living marine catfish family, which is documented by the teleost otolith (ear-bone) genus *Vorhisia*.

Among marine reptiles, hard-shelled sea turtles had increased in diversity (Table 1) and were represented by the genera *Euclastes, Peritresius*, and *Prionochelys*, while the leatherback sea turtle line was represented by the genera *Pneumatoarthrus, Neptunochelys*, and *Corsochelys*. [120] The long-neck plesiosaurs (Figure 38) were still present and represented with certainty by the large species *Cimoliasaurus magnus*.[121]

Hyposaurus

Mosasaurus

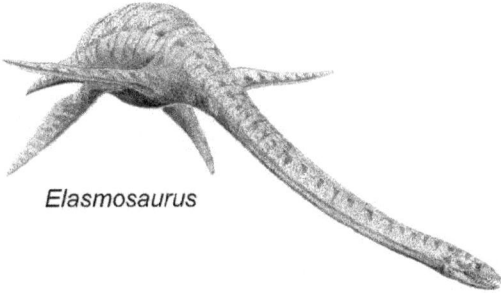

Elasmosaurus

1 m

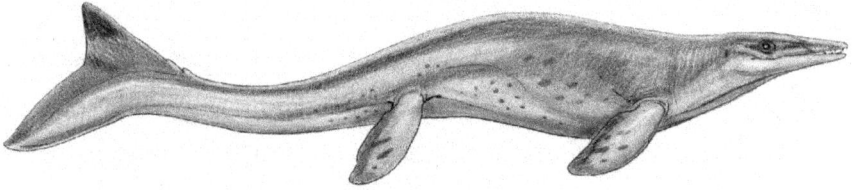

Tylosaurus

Figure 38 – Marine reptiles known from the Virginia region during the Maastrichtian stage of the Cretaceous. Sources for figure shown in Appendix 2.

The marine crocodilian *Thoracosaurus neocessariensis* persisted from the Campanian and had been joined by another marine crocodilian new to the waters of the western Atlantic, *Hyposaurus rogersii*.[122] *Hyposaurus* and *Thoracosaurus* were among the few animals that survived from the Cretaceous into the Paleocene.

Mosasaurs continued to thrive and dominate the apex marine predator roles. They were represented in Atlantic coastal waters by species of *Halisaurus, Liodon, Mosasaurus, Platycarpus, Plioplatecarpus,* and *Prognathodon*.[123] Although two Campanian mosasaur species had disappeared by the Maastrichtian and presumably gone extinct, four new species appeared to replace them. Ultimately, the overall diversity of mosasaurs actually increased from the Campanian to the Maastrichtian.

❖ ❖ ❖

The Mesozoic Era ended due to two major catastrophes that befell planet Earth at the same time. One was a major episode of volcanism that produced a massive thickness of basalt exposed today in India and known as the Deccan Traps. This volcanic event began about 66.3 million years ago, roughly two hundred thousand years before the end of the Maastricthian, and continued into the early Paleocene epoch of the Cenozoic Era (Figure 2). This event was in many ways similar to the event that broke up Pangaea at the end of the Triassic Period. Both events destabilized the global climate by introducing large volumes of carbon dioxide and volcanic ash into the air and, through weathering of the newly formed basaltic rocks, altered the chemistry of the oceans. As in the Triassic event, the results of this massive volcanism were extremely detrimental to the global environment. The most recent estimate, based on work done in Antarctica, indicates that the Deccan Trap event probably accounted for slightly less than half of the total observed marine extinctions that occurred at the end of the Cretaceous.[124]

Figure 39 – Artist's rendition of the impact of the Chicxulub asteroid at the end of the Mesozoic Era in what is today Yucatan, Mexico. Source for figure shown in Appendix 2.

Had the Deccan Trap event been the sum of the climatic and environmental perturbations that affected world climate at the end of the Cretaceous, life likely would have recovered and gone on much as it had before. But this was not to be. About two hundred thousand years after the Deccan Trap event began, 66.1 million years ago, a gigantic asteroid perhaps as much as ten miles in diameter slammed into what is now the Yucatan Peninsula in Mexico.[125] This impact (Figures 35 and 39) created the Chicxulub impact crater, which was about two hundred miles in diameter and probably released as much energy as a billion or so nuclear bombs. Even worse, the asteroid landed in the middle of a thick sequence of nearshore marine rocks that consisted of miles-thick limestone and gypsum-laden rocks. The gypsum in these rocks, composed of calcium sulfate, almost instantly vaporized to form immense clouds of sulfate minerals. Once introduced into the air, they would have been highly toxic to life on their own and, as these gases were washed slowly from the atmosphere, would have created a vast volume of acid rain.[126] Modern birds are more likely than mammals to be killed by high concentrations of sulfate compounds in the air, which gave rise to the old practice of bringing canaries into coal mines. If the canaries died, it was time for the miners to get out before they also died from poisonous fumes. What is most important to our story here is that birds are the only direct dinosaur descendants that survived the end-Cretaceous extinction event. In all likelihood, the dinosaurs that died in the end-Cretaceous disaster were even more sensitive to sulfates in the air than modern birds and were thus even less capable of surviving this kind of disaster.

Heat that spread from the impact site appears to have caused flash fires across huge areas beyond the crater site in North and South America. This is indicated by an abundance of charcoal soot in strata that were accumulating at the time of the Chicxulub impact, and by a big increase in the abundance of fern spores immediately above the impact stratum. Together, these two observations suggest that much of the world's vegetation was burnt to the ground during the Chicxulub impact event, and that afterward, ferns, which readily send up shoots from underground root systems that are protected from fires, came briefly to dominate the western hemisphere ground cover. Only after this were sheltered pockets of surviving higher plant groups able to spread from protected areas and re-establish their dominance in the vast areas where they had been completely killed off. The carbon dioxide and sulfate minerals introduced into the atmosphere, soot released in flash fires, acid rain, and vast volumes of impact-generated dust that obscured light from the sun conspired to plunge the world into a crisis worse than any other documented in the history of our planet with the sole exception of the Great End-Permian Extinction Event.

Strata from the very end of the Mesozoic are not exposed in Virginia nor in any of the other Atlantic Coast states that include parts of the Atlantic Coastal Plain. At that time, sea levels were somewhat lower than today, so the East Coast region including the western part of the Atlantic Coastal Plain was undergoing erosion and not deposition. There is, however, a time-continuous section across the Cretaceous-Paleogene boundary that has been discovered in a deep core taken near the Atlantic coast in New Jersey. At the Cretaceous-Paleogene boundary in this core, there is a compacted clay layer that represents fallout ash from the Chicxulub impact event. Microtectites and other impact debris of small size, along with anomalously high levels of iridium within this layer, all demonstrate that it is from the Chicxulub meteor impact event and not from some volcanic eruption.[127]

In southern Alabama, which is a part of the Gulf Coastal Plain, there is an outcrop above modern sea level where the Cretaceous-Paleogene boundary layer is exposed and readily visible to visitors.[128] Here, closer to the impact site in Yucatan, a chaotic layer of gravel and mudballs of very varied sizes is exposed. This deposit is widespread in the Gulf Coast region, but it is mostly covered by vegetation and only easily accessible for viewing in a few places. This deposit was formed by a tidal wave that surged outward from the impact site in Yucatan and then, when it reached the southern shores of North America, surged northward over the low-lying lands there for many tens or perhaps even hundreds of miles. Then, as its energy waned, the tsunami waters washed back toward the Gulf of Mexico. The return flow of this surge left a chaotic debris layer as a testament to its passing. In this case as well, microtectites and other distinctive impact debris are mixed in with the gravel bed, showing that these deposits were derived from an extraterrestrial asteroid impact event and not from a volcanic eruption or an earthquake-induced tsunami event.

Together, these two great environmental disasters caused the extinction of about 75% of all plant and animal life on Earth. The southeastern United States, which was relatively close to the impact site, must have been exceptionally devastated. All of the varied dinosaurs and pterosaurs living at that time were killed off, along with a great many of the smaller mammals, birds, reptiles, and amphibians that lived along with them. Many of the marine sharks and bony fishes that were common in the surrounding Late Cretaceous seas were also exterminated, as were all of the plesiosaurs, mosasaurs, and the last surviving lungfishes and lobe-fin fishes living in and around North America. Both on the land and in the sea, life in the Virginia region and elsewhere had been profoundly changed forever.

For a while, some of the smaller and more aquatic inhabitants of Appalachia were able to survive, notably some of the turtles and crocodilians. But most of these endemic species that survived this event persisted for only another few millions of years before dying off toward the end of the early Paleocene Danian stage (Figure 2). By the middle of the Paleocene, a number of new vertebrate species arrived from western North America, and these displaced the last of the endemic species of Appalachia.[129] With their extinction, the last remaining remnants of the unique fauna that had arisen on the microcontinent of Appalachia disappeared forever from the fossil record. From this time forward, the age of mammals began in earnest, and a very new and different world order began to take shape.

EPILOGUE

WHERE TO SEE MESOZOIC FOSSILS AND EXHIBITS RELATED TO VIRGINIA

I n the western United States, a great many Mesozoic strata are widely exposed. From them, a large number of dinosaur and other Mesozoic vertebrate fossils have been collected and put on exhibit. All of these places are well worth a visit when traveling out west. In the eastern United States, however, far fewer exposures of Mesozoic strata exist, so much less material is available to be found and collected. This has resulted in far fewer places for visitors to see what remains from the eastern North American Mesozoic world.

Within Virginia, the best exhibit is at the Virginia Museum of Natural History in Martinsville, Virginia. A nice skeleton of *Acrocanthosaurus* is on exhibit, along with dinosaur materials from western parts of the United States. There is a diorama showing Triassic life, and there also are some exhibits of fossils from the Danville Triassic Basin, including some of the Triassic insect material that is among the best preserved in the world.

At the United States Geological Survey headquarters in Reston, there are dinosaur footprints exhibited on the floor of the lobby that came from the Triassic part of the Culpeper Basin. These footprints include the dinosaur footprints *Kayentapus minor* and *Grallator tuberosus*. There is also an exact replica of a very large Late Cretaceous *Tyrannosauripus* footprint from the western United States.

In the town of Culpeper, at the Museum of Culpeper History, there is a large and detailed photograph of the Culpeper Quarry footprint layer, taken when it was well exposed and under study, along with a slab of rock that contains two successive footprints of *Kayentapus minor* that came from this layer in the quarry. In Charlottesville, at the library of the Virginia Department of Mines, Minerals, and Energy, there is a display cabinet with Jurassic fish and a Jurassic footprint of *Kayentapus minor* that came from Oak Hill Estate in Loudoun County. For the active younger crowd, Dinosaur Land at White Post near Winchester and Jerrassic Park—Metal Dinosaur Park in Virginia Beach are good day outings to stir their imaginations.

In nearby states, the North Carolina Museum of Natural Sciences in Raleigh has a nice exhibit on North Carolina dinosaurs and related animals. From the Early Cretaceous, there is a life-size skeleton of *Acrocanthosaurus*, a life-size model of *Astrodon* (they prefer to call it by the Texas name *Pleurocoelus*), and life-size models of pterosaurs circling overhead. There is also a gallery displaying Late Cretaceous and Late Triassic dinosaur and other vertebrate remains found in North Carolina, along with dioramas providing insight into the world in which these animals lived. Other dinosaur exhibits can be found at the North Carolina Museum of Natural Sciences branch in Whiteville, the Schiele Museum of Natural History and Planetarium in Gastonia, and the Greensboro Science Center.

In Washington, D.C., the Smithsonian has an impressive new dinosaur hall that opened in June of 2019. In Laurel, Maryland, there is the Laurel Dinosaur Park, which has a diorama of what the area looked like in the Early Cretaceous and a number of specimens on exhibit found at this site. On the first and third Saturdays of every month, it is possible to volunteer to help look for new fossil material that is still being found in this park. Also worth a visit is the Maryland Science Center in Baltimore, where visitors can see more than two dozen dinosaur skeletons.

Farther afield to the north, the Academy of Natural Sciences of Drexel University in Philadelphia, Pennsylvania, and the New Jersey State Museum in Trenton, New Jersey, both have nice exhibits of dinosaur material, including some of the specimens from New Jersey mentioned in this book. For excellent wide-ranging dinosaur exhibits not emphasizing local dinosaurs, but not so far away as the western museums and parks, the American Museum of Natural History in New York City and the Carnegie Museum in Pittsburgh, Pennsylvania, are both well worth a visit for their superb dinosaur and other fossil exhibits.

REFERENCES CITED

Ash, S.R., and Creber, G.T., 2000, The Late Triassic *Araucarioxylon ari-zonicum* trees of the Petrified Forest National Park, Arizona, USA: Palaeontology, v. 43, part 1, p. 15-28.

Baird, D., 1967, Age of fossil birds from the greensands of New Jersey: The Auk, v. 84, p. 260-262. [*Telmatornis*]

Baird, D., 1984, Evidence of giant protostegid sea-turtles in the Cretaceous of New Jersey: The Mosasaur, v. 2, p. 135-140. [*Pneumatoarthrus*]

Baird, D., 1986a, Upper Cretaceous reptiles from the Severn Formation of Maryland: The Mosasaur, v. 3, p. 63-85. [*Cimoliosaurus*, Had-rosauridae indet., *Halisaurus, Mosasaurus, Ornithomimus, Osteopygis, Peritresius, Prognathodon, "Trionyx"*]

Baird, D. 1986b, Some Upper Triassic reptiles, footprints and an amphib-ian from New Jersey: The Mosasaur, v.. 3, p. 125–135. [*Apatopus, Gwyneddichnium, Hypsognathus, Procolophonichnium, Rutiodon, Stegomus*]

Baird, D., 1989, Medial Cretaceous carnivorous dinosaur and footprints from New Jersey: The Mosasaur, v. 4, p. 53-63. [cf. *Irenesauripus*, carnosaur aff. *Appalachiosaurus*]

Baird, D., and Galton, P.M., 1981, Pterosaur bones from the Upper Cre-taceous of Delaware: Journal of Vertebrate Paleontology, v. 1, no. 1, p. 67-71. [*Deinosuchus, Holops* (= *Thoracosaurus*), *Mosasaurus, Pteran-odon, "Trionyx"*]

Baird, D., and Horner, J.R., 1979, Cretaceous dinosaurs of North Caro-lina: Brimleyana, v. 1, no. 2, p. 1-28. [*Asterocanthus, Borealosuchus* (= *Leidyosuchus*), *Brachyrhizodus, Deinosuchus, Dryptosaurus, Hyps-ibema, Ischyrhiza, Ornithomimus, Paralbula, Plateocarpus, Pycnodus, Scapanorhyncus, Squalicorax, Taphrosphys, "Trionyx," Tylosaurus*]

Berry, E.W., 1911a, The Lower Cretaceous floras of the world, p. 99-152 *in* Maryland Geological Survey, Lower Cretaceous: Baltimore, Johns Hopkins Press, 622 p.

Berry, E.W., 1911b, The flora of the Raritan Formation: New Jersey Geological Survey, Department of Conservation and Development, v. 3, 233 p., 29 pls.

Berry, E.W., 1916, The Raritan flora, p. 199-203 *in* Maryland Geological Survey, Upper Cretaceous Text: Baltimore, Johns Hopkins Press, 578 p.

Bock, W., 1945, A new small reptile from the Triassic of Pennsylvania: Academy of Natural Sciences of Philadelphia, Notula Naturae 154, p. 1-8. [*Gwyneddosaurus*]

Brownstein, C.D., 2017, Description of Arundel Clay ornithomimosaur material and a reinterpretation of *Nedcolbertia justinhofmanni* as an "Ostrich Dinosaur": biogeographic implications: PeerJ, v. 5, e3110.

Brownstein, C.D., 2018a, The biogeography and ecology of the Cretaceous non-avian dinosaurs of Appalachia: Palaeontologia Electronica 21.1.5A.1-56. [*Hadrosaurus, Ornithomimus, Dryptosaurus*, nodosaurid]

Brownstein, C.D., 2018b, Large basal tyrannosauroids from the Maastrichtian and terrestrial vertebrate diversity in the shadow of the K-Pg extinction: The Mosasaur, v. 10, p. 105-115 [*Dryptosaurus*, cf. *Appalachiosaurus*]

Campbell, M.R., and Kimball, K.K., 1923, The Deep River coal field of North Carolina: North Carolina Geological and Economic Survey Bulletin 33: p. 1–95.

Carpenter, K., and Tidwell, V., 2005, Reassessment of the Early Cretaceous sauropod *Astrodon johnstoni* Leidy 1865 (Titanosauriformes) *in* Carpenter, K., and Tidwell, V., eds., Thunder Lizards: The Sauropodomorph Dinosaurs: Indiana University Press. p. 38–77.

Case, G.R., 1979, Cretaceous selachians from the Peedee Formation (Late Maastrichtian) of Duplin County, North Carolina: Brimleyana, v. 2, p. 77-89. [*Cretolamna, Hybodus, Ischyrhyza, Odontaspis, Plicatolamna, Rhombodus, Scapanorhyncus, Squalicorax*]

Case, G.R., Cook, T.D., Sadorf, E.M., and Shannon, K.R., 2017, A late Maastrichtian assemblage from the Peedee Formation of North Carolina, USA: Vertebrate Anatomy, Morphology, Palaeontology, v. 3, p. 63-80. [*Anomotodon, Cantioscyllium, Carcharias, Cretalamna, Dasyatis, Heterodontus, Ischyrhiza, Notidanodon, Odontaspis, Palaeogaleus, Plicatoscyllium, Pseudocorax, Ptycotrygon, Raja, Rhinobatos, Rhombodus, Sclerorhynchus, Serratolamna, Squalicorax, Squalus*]

Chinnery, B.J., Lipka, T.R., Kirkland, J.I., Parrish, M.J., and Brett-Surman, M.K., 1998, Neoceratopsian teeth from the Lower to Middle Cretaceous of North America *in* Lucas, S.G., Kirkland, J.I., and Estep, J.W., eds., Lower and Middle Cretaceous Terrestrial Ecosystems: New Mexico Museum of Natural History and Science Bulletin 14, p. 297-302.

Clark, W.B., 1916, The Upper Cretaceous deposits of Maryland, p. 23-119 *in* Maryland Geological Survey, Upper Cretaceous Text: Baltimore, Johns Hopkins Press, 578 p.

Clark, W.B., Miller, B.L., Berry, E.W., and Watson, T.L., 1912, The physiography and geology of the Coastal Plain Province of Virginia: Virginia Geological Survey Bulletin, v. 4, p. 1–274.

Colbert, E.H., and Imbrie, J., 1956, Triassic metoposaurid amphibians: Bulletin of the American Museum of Natural History, v. 110, art. 6, p. 399-452. [*Dictyocephalus*]

Cope, E.D., 1871, Observations on the distribution of certain extinct Vertebrata in North Carolina: Proceedings of the American Philosophical Society, v. 12: p. 210-216. [*Hadrosaurus, Hypsibema, Zatomus*]

Cornet, B., and Olsen, P. E., 1990, Early to Middle Carnian (Triassic) flora and fauna of the Richmond and Taylorsville basins, Virginia and Maryland, U.S.A.: Virginia Museum of Natural History, Guidebook, no. 1, 83 p. [*Dictyopyge, Cionichthys, Tanaocrossus*, Coelacanthiformes, *Doswellia*, Phytosauridae indet., Rauisuchidae indet.]

Crane, C.D., 2011, Vertebrate paleontology and taphonomy of the Late Cretaceous (Campanian) Bladen Formation, Bladen County, North Carolina: M.S. thesis, East Carolina University, 208 p. [*Albanerpeton, Albula, Anomoedus, Borealosuchus, Borodinopristis, Bothremys, Brachyrhizodus, Chedighaii, Cimolomys, Coniophis, Cretolamna,*

Dasyatis, Deinosuchus, Dromaeosauridae, Elasmosauridae, *Enchodus, Galeorhinus, Ginglymostoma, Hadrodus,* Hadrosauridae, *Hybodus, Hypsibema, Ischyrhiza, Lepisosteus, Lonchidion, Ornithomimus, Paralbula, Protoplatyrhina, Ptychotrygon, Rhinobatos, Rhombus, Scapanorhynchus, Schizorhiza, Squalicorax, Squatina, "Trionyx," Tylosaurus,* Tyrannosauridae, *Xiphactinus*]

Cousminer, H.L., and Steinkraus, W.E., 1988, Chapter 7 - Biostratigraphy of the COST G-2 well (Georges Bank): a record of Late Triassic synrift evaporite deposition; Liassic doming; and mid-Jurassic to Miocene postrift marine sedimentation *in* Mannspeizer, W., ed., Triassic-Jurassic Rifting: Continental Breakup and the Origin of the Atlantic Ocean and Passive Margins, Developments in Geotectonics, v. 22, p. 167-184.

D'Emic, M.D., 2013, Revision of the sauropod dinosaurs of the Lower Cretaceous Trinity Group, southern USA, with the description of a new genus: Journal of Systematic Palaeontology, v. 11, no. 6, p. 707–726. [*Astrodon*]

D'Emic, M.D., and Foreman, B.Z., 2012, The beginning of the sauropod dinosaur hiatus in North America: insights from the Lower Cretaceous Cloverly Formation of Wyoming: Journal of Vertebrate Paleontology, v. 32, no. 4, p. 883-902.

Denton, R.K., Jr., and O'Neill, R.C., 1995, *Prototeius stageri,* gen. et sp. nov., a new teiid lizard from the Upper Cretaceous Marshalltown Formation of New Jersey, with a preliminary phylogenetic revision of the Teiidae: Journal of Vertebrate Paleontology, v. 15, no. 2, p. 235-253.

Denton, R.K., Jr., and O'Neill, R.C., 1998, *Parrisia neocesariensis,* a new batrachosauroidid salamander and other amphibians from the Campanian of eastern North America: Journal of Vertebrate Paleontology, v. 18, no. 3, p. 484–494.

Denton, R.K., Jr., & O'Neill, R.C., 2008, A Revision of the Squamate Fauna of the Ellisdale Dinosaur Site, Upper Cretaceous (Campanian) Marshalltown Formation of New Jersey: Journal of Vertebrate Paleontology, v. 28, no. 3 (supplement), p. 71A.

Denton, R.K., Jr., & O'Neill, R. C., 2010, A new stagodontid metatherian from the Campanian of New Jersey and its implications for a lack of east-west dispersal routes in the Late Cretaceous of North America: Journal of Vertebrate Paleontology, v. 30, no. 3 (supplement).

Dickas, A.B., 2018, 101 American Fossil Sites You've Gotta See: Missoula, Montana, Mountain Press Publishing Company, 254 p.

Doyle, J.A., and Hickey L.J., 1976, Pollen and leaves from the mid-Cretaceous Potomac Group and their bearing on early angiosperm evolution *in* Beck, C.B., ed., Origin and Early Evolution of Angiosperms: New York, Columbia University Press. p. 139-206.

Doyle, J.A., and Robbins, E.I., 1977, Angiosperm pollen zonation of the continental Cretaceous of the Atlantic Coastal Plain and its application to deep wells in the Salisbury Embayment: Palynology, vol. 1, p. 43-78.

Emmons, E., 1856, Geological report of the midland counties of North Carolina: North Carolina Geological Survey, Raleigh, 351 p.

Emmons, E., 1860, Manual of geology, Second edition: New York, viii + 297 p.

Farke, A.A., and Phillips, G.E., 2017, The first reported ceratopsid dinosaur from eastern North America (Owl Creek Formation, Upper Cretaceous, Mississippi, USA): PeerJ, 5:e3342. https://doi.org/10.7717/peerj.3342.

Fenton, C.L., and Fenton, M.A., 1958, The Fossil Book: A Record of Prehistoric Life: Garden City, Doubleday & Company, Inc., 482 p.

Foster, J., 2007, Jurassic West: The Dinosaurs of the Morrison Formation and Their World. Indiana University Press, 389 p.

Fraser, N. C., and Olsen, P. E., 1996, A new dinosauromorph ichnogenus from the Triassic of Virginia. Jeffersoniana, no. 7, p. 1-17. [*Banisterobates*]

Fraser, N.C., Grimaldi, D.A., Olsen, P.E. and Axsmith, B., 1996, A Triassic lagerstätte from eastern North America: Nature, v. 380, no. 6575, p. 615-619.

Fraser, N.C., Olsen, P. E., Dooley, A.C. Jr., and Ryan, T.R., 2007, A new gliding tetrapod (Diapsida: ?Archosauromorpha) from the Upper

Triassic (Carnian) of Virginia: Journal of Vertebrate Paleontology, v. 27, no. 2, p. 261–265. [*Mecistotrachelos*]

Frederickson, J.A., Lipka, T.R., and Cifelli, R.L., 2016, A new species of the lungfish *Ceratodus* (Dipnoi) from the Early Cretaceous of the eastern U.S.A.: Journal of Vertebrate Paleontology, DOI:10.1080/0 2724634.2016.1136316.

Frederickson, J.A., Lipka, T.R., and Cifelli, R.L., 2018, Faunal composition and paleoenvironment of the Arundel Clay (Potomac Formation; Early Cretaceous), Maryland, USA: Palaeontologia Electronica 21.2.31A 1-24. https://doi.org/10.26879/847palaeo-electronica. org/content/2018/2290-arundel-fauna-of-maryland-usa [*Acrocanthosaurus, Argillomys, Arundelconodon, Arundelemys, Astrodon*, Bernissartiidae, *Ceratodus, Deinonychus, Egertonodus, Glyptops*, Goniopholidae, *Hybodus, Lepidotes, Naomichelys*, Neoceratopsia, Ornithomimosauria, Pholidosauridae, *Priconodon, Richardoestesia*, Vidalamiinae]

Gallagher, W.B., 1993, The Cretaceous-Tertiary mass extinction event in the North Atlantic Coastal Plain: The Mosasaur, v. 5, p. 75-154. [*Neptunochelys, Corsochelys, Osteopygis, Titanopteryx (= Arambourgiania), Halisaurus, Liodon, Mosasaurus, Plioplatecarpus, Prognathodon, Telmatornis*]

Gallagher, W.B., Parris, D.C., and Spamer, E.E., 1986, Paleontology, biostratigraphy, and depositional environments of the Cretaceous-Tertiary transition in the New Jersey Coastal Plain: The Mosasaur, v. 3, p. 1-35 [*Adocus, Anomoeodus, Bothremys, Brachychampsa, Brachyrhizodus, Cimoliasaurus, Corsochelys, Cretolamna, Cylindracanthus, Deinosuchus, Dryptosaurus, Enchodus, Hadrosaurus, Hybodus, Hypsibema, Ischyodus, Ischyrhiza, Leidysuchus (= Borealosuchus), Mosasaurus, Odontaspis, Ornithomimus, Osteopygis, Paralbula, Peritresius, Platycarpus, Prognathodon, Rhombodus, Scapanorhynchus, Squalicorax, Squatina, Stephanodus, Taphrosphys, "Trionyx," Xiphactinus*]

Garcia, W., and Hippensteel, S., 2011, New vertebrate material from the Peedee Formation of Elizabethtown, NC and the Severn Formation of Bowie, MD and the shallow marine vertebrate fauna of the upper Campanian-upper Maastrichtian of eastern North America: Geological Society of America Abstracts with Programs, v. 43, no. 5, p.

83. [*Cretolamna, Enchodus, Odontaspis, Osteopygis, Scapanorhyncus, Squalicorax, "Trionyx"*]

Gore, P.J.W., and Traverse, A., 1986, Triassic notostracans in the Newark Supergroup, Culpeper Basin, northern Virginia: Journal of Paleontology, v. 60, no. 5, p. 1086-1096.

Grandstaff, B.S., Parris, D.C., Denton, R.K., Jr., and Gallagher, W.B., 1992, *Alphadon* (Marsupialia) and Multituberculata (Allotheria) in the Cretaceous of eastern North America: Journal of Vertebrate Paleontology, v. 12, no. 2, p. 217-222.

Green, J., Schneider, V., Schweizer, M., and Clarke, J., 2005, New Evidence for non-*Placerias* dicynodonts in the Late Triassic (Carnian-Norian) of North America: Journal of Vertebrate Paleontology, v. 23, supplement to no. 3, p. 65A-66A. [aff. *Placerias*]

Hajzer, F., Gudni, F., Grandstaff, B.S., and Parris, D.C., 2018, The second fossil lungfish tooth plate from the Cretaceous of New Jersey, U.S.A.: The Mosasaur, v. 10, p. 79-83. [*Ceratodus*, early Maastrichtian]

Hansen, H.J., 1992, Stratigraphy of Upper Cretaceous and Tertiary sediments in a core-hole drilled near Chesterville, Kent County, Maryland: Maryland Geological Survey Open-File Report 93-02-7, p. 1-38, 4 pls.

Hansen, H.J., and Drummond, D.D., 1994, Upper Cretaceous and Tertiary stratigraphy of core-hole Ken-Bf 180 clarifies aquifer nomenclature in Kent County, Maryland *in* Schultz, A.P., and Rader, E.K., eds., Studies in eastern energy and the environment: Virginia Division of Mineral Resources Publication 132, p. 50-56.

Harrell, T.L., Jr., Gibson, M.A., and Langston, W. Jr., 2016, A cervical vertebra of *Arambourgiania philadelphiae* (Pterosauria, Azhdarchidae) from the Late Campanian micaceous facies of the Coon Creek Formation in McNairy County, Tennessee, USA; Bulletin of the Alabama Museum of Natural History, v. 33, p. 94–103.

Harris, J.D., 1998, Large, Early Cretaceous theropods in North America *in* Lucas, S.G., Kirkland, J.I., and Estep, J.W., eds., Lower and Middle Cretaceous Terrestrial Ecosystems: New Mexico Museum of Natural History and Science Bulletin 14. p. 225–228. [*Acrocanthosaurus*]

Hartstein, E.F., and Decina, L.E., 1986, A new Severn Formation (early middle Maastrichtian, Late Cretaceous) locality in Prince Georges County, Maryland: The Mosasaur, v. 3, p. 87-95. [*Anomoeodus, Cretolamna, Enchodus, Hypotodus, Ischyrhyza, Myliobatis, Odontaspis, Squalicorax, Squatina, Stephanodus*]

Hartstein, E.F., and Lauginiger, E.M., 1983, A guide to fossil sharks, skates, and rays from the Chesapeake And Delaware Canal area, Delaware: Delaware Geological Survey, University of Delaware, Newark, 63 p.

Hartstein, E.F., Decina, L.E., and Keil, R.F., 1999, A Late Cretaceous (Severn Formation) vertebrate assemblage from Bowie, Maryland: The Mosasaur, v. 6, p. 17-23. [Albulidae indet., cf. *Allognathosuchus, Anomoedus, Bottosaurus, Carcharias, Chiloscyllium, Cimoliosaurus, Cretolamna, Cylindracanthus, Dasyatis, Deinosuchus, Egertonia, Enchodus, Ewingia, Galeorhinus, Ginglymostoma, Hadrodus,* Hadrosauridae indet., *Heterodontus, Hybodus, Ischyodus, Ischyrhyza, Lepisosteus, Mosasaurus, Myliobatis, Odontaspis,* Ornithomimidae indet. , *Paralbula, Peritresius, Plicatoscyllium, Pseudohypolophus, Ptychotrygon, Raja, Rhinobatos, Rhombodus, Serratolamna, Squalicorax, Squatina, Thoracosaurus, "Trionyx"*]

Heckert, A.B., Mitchell. J.S., Schneider, V., and Olsen, P.E., 2012, Diverse new microvertebrate assemblage from the Upper Triassic Cumnock Formation, Sanford subbasin, North Carolina, USA: Journal of Paleontology, v. 86, no. 2, p. 368-390. [*Arganodus, Colognathus,* Sphenodontidae indet., *Galtonia, Crosbysaurus, Uatchitodon, Revueltosaurus, Boreogomphodon, Microconodon*]

Heckert, A.B., Schneider, V.P., Fraser, N.C., and Webb, R.A., 2015, A new aetosaur (Archosauria, Suchia) from the Upper Triassic Pekin Formation, Deep River Basin, North Carolina, U.S.A., and its implications for early aetosaur evolution: Journal of Vertebrate Paleontology. v. 35: e881831. doi:10.1080/02724634.2014.881831 [*Coahomasuchus, Lucasuchus, Gorgetosuchus*]

Holmes, R.B., and Sues, H.D., 2000, A partial skeleton of the basal mosasaur *Halisaurus platyspondylus* from the Severn Formation (Upper Cretaceous: Maastrichtian) of Maryland: Journal of Paleontology, v. 74, no. 2, p. 309-315.

Holtz, T.R., Jr., 2008, Dinosaurs: The Most Complete, Up-to-Date Encyclopedia for Dinosaur Lovers of All Ages: New York, Random House, 428 p.

Huddleston, R.W., and Savoie, K.M., 1983, Teleostean otoliths from the Late Cretaceous (Maastrichtian age) Severn Formation of Maryland: Proceedings of the Biological Society of Washington, v. 96, no. 4, p. 658-663. [*Vorhisia*, Apagonidae, and 10 other families of teleostean otoliths]

Huene, F. von, 1948, Notes on *Gwyneddosaurus*: American Journal of Science, v. 246, no. 4, p. 208-213.

Iturralde-Vinent, M.A., and Izquierdo, Y.C., 2015, Catalogue of Late Jurassic vertebrate (Pisces, Reptilian) specimens from western Cuba: Paleontologia Mexicana, v. 3, no. 5, p. 24-39.

Kent, B.W., 1994, Fossil sharks of the Chesapeake Bay region: Columbia, Maryland, Egan Rees & Boyer, Inc., 146 p. [*Cantioscyllium, Charcharias, Chiloscyllium, Cretodus, Cretolamna, Galeorhinus, Ginglymostoma, Hybodus, Lissodus, Odontaspis, Paranomotodon, Pseudocorax, Scapanorhynchus, Squalicorax, Squatina*]

Key, M.M., Jr., and Delano, H.L., 1993, Stop 6: The Triassic dinosaurs and the Trostle Quarry, p. 28-34 *in* Britcher, R.W., ed., Guidebook for the 12th Annual Field Trip of the Harrisburg Area Geological Society (May 22, 1993) - South Mountain and the Triassic in Adams County: Harrisburg Area Geological Society, Harrisburg, Pennsylvania, 41 p. [*Pentasauropus*]

Kozur, H.W., and Weems, R.E., 2010, The biostratigraphic importance of conchostracans in the continental Triassic of the northern hemisphere *in* Lucas, S.G., ed., The Triassic timescale: Geological Society, London, Special Publication 334, p. 315-417.

Kranz, P.M., 1998, Mostly dinosaurs: a review of the vertebrates of the Potomac Group (Aptian Arundel Formation), USA *in* Lucas, S.G., Kirkland, J.E., and Estep, J.W., eds., Lower and Middle Cretaceous terrestrial ecosystems: New Mexico Museum of Natural History and Science Bulletin 14, p. 235-238. [*Ceratodus, Glyptops, Hybodus, Naomichelys?, Tenontosaurus*, crocodilia indet.]

Krause, D.W., and Baird, D., 1979, Late Cretaceous mammals east of the North American western interior seaway: Journal of Paleontology, v. 53, no. 3, p.562-565. [multituberculate femur from the Maastrichtian of New Jersey]

Lauginiger, E.M., 1984, An upper Campanian vertebrate fauna from the Chesapeake and Delaware Canal, Delaware: The Mosasaur, v. 2, p. 141-150. [*Anomoeodus, Brachyrhizodus, Clidastes, Cylindracanthus, Enchodus, Ginglymostoma, Globidens, Hybodus, Hypotodus* (= *Odontaspis*), *Ischyodus, Ischyrhyza, Leidyosuchus* (= *Borealosuchus*), *Lepisosteus, Lonchidion, Odontaspis, Paralbula, Paranomotodon, Plicatolamna, Pseudocorax, Pseudohypolophus, Ptychotrygon, Rhinobatos, Rhombodus, Sclerorhynchus, Scapanorhynchus, Squalicorax, Squatina, Stephanodus, "Trionyx," Xiphactinus*]

Lee, K.Y., and Froelich, A.J., 1989, Triassic-Jurassic stratigraphy of the Culpeper and Barboursville basins, Virginia and Maryland: U.S. Geological Survey Professional Paper 1472, p. 1–52.

Leidy, J., 1856, Notice of remains of extinct vertebrated animals discovered by Professor E. Emmons: Proceedings of the Academy of Natural Sciences of Philadelphia, v. 8, p. 255-257.

LeTourneau, P.M., 2003, Tectonic and climatic controls on the stratigraphic architecture of the Late Triassic Taylorsville Basin, Virginia and Maryland *in* LeTourneau, P.M. and Olsen, P.E., The great rift valleys of Pangea in eastern North America: New York, Columbia University Press, p. 12-58.

Lindholm, R.C., 1979, Geologic history and stratigraphy of the Triassic-Jurassic Culpeper Basin, Virginia: Geological Society of America Bulletin, v. 90, p. 1702–1736.

Lipka, T.R., 1998, The affinities of the enigmatic theropods of the Arundel Clay facies (Aptian), Potomac Formation, Atlantic Coastal Plain of Maryland *in* Lucas, S.G., Kirkland, J.I., and Estep, J.W., eds., Lower and Middle Cretaceous Terrestrial Ecosystems: New Mexico Museum of Natural History and Science Bulletin 14. p. 229–234. [*Acrocanthosaurus*]

Lipka, T.R., Therrien, F., Weishampel, D.B., Jamniczky, H.A., Joyce, W.G., Colbert, M.W., and Brinkman, D.B., 2006, A new turtle from the Arundel Clay Facies (Potomac Formation, Early Cretaceous) of Maryland, U.S.A.: Journal of Vertebrate Paleontology, v. 26, no. 2, p. 300-307. [*Arundelemys*]

Liu, J., Schneider, V.P., Olsen, P.E., 2017, The postcranial skeleton of *Boreogomphodon* (Cynodontia: Traversodontidae) from the Upper Triassic of North Carolina, USA and the comparison with other traversodontids: PeerJ, v. 5:e3521 [also *Plinthogomphodon* which is synonymized with *Boreogomphodon*]

Lockley, M., Harris, J.D., and Mitchell, L., 2008, A global overview of pterosaur ichnology: tracksite distribution in space and time: Zitteliana. v. B28, p. 187-198.

Longrich, N.R., 2016, A ceratopsian dinosaur from the Late Cretaceous of eastern North America, and implications for dinosaur biogeography. Cretaceous Research, 57, 199-207. DOI: 10.1016/j.cretres.2015.08.004 [Leptoceratopsidae]

Lovelace, D.M., Hartman, S.A., and Wahl, W.R., 2007, Morphology of a specimen of *Supersaurus* (Dinosauria, Sauropoda) from the Morrison Formation of Wyoming, and a re-evaluation of diplodocid phylogeny: Arquivos do Museu Nacional, v. 65, no. 4, p. 527–544.

Lucas, S.G., 1998, Global Triassic tetrapod biostratigraphy and biochronology: Palaeogeography, Palaeoclimatology, Palaeoecology, v. 143, p. 347-384.

Lucas, S.G., 2010, The Triassic timescale based on nonmarine tetrapod biostratigraphy and biochronology *in* Lucas, S.G., ed., The Triassic timescale: Geological Society, London, Special Publication 334, p. 447-500.

Lucas, S.G., and Tanner, L.H., 2018a, Record of the Carnian wet episode in strata of the Chinle Group, western USA: Journal of the Geological Society, v. 175, no. 6, p. 1004-1011.

Lucas, S.G., and Tanner, L.H., 2018b, The missing mass extinction at the Triassic-Jurassic boundary *in* The Late Triassic World: Springer, Cham, p. 721-785.

Lyell, C., 1839-33, Principles of geology, being an attempt to explain the former changes of the Earth's surface, by reference to causes now in operation: London, John Murray, 3 vols.

Lyell, C., 1845, Travels in North America: London, John Murray, 2 vols.

Lyell, C., 1849, A second visit to the United States of North America: London, John Murray, 2 vols.

Malinconico, M.L., 2003, Estimates of eroded strata using borehole vitrinite reflectance data, Triassic Taylorsville rift basin, Virginia: Implications for duration of synrift sedimentation and evidence of structural inversion *in* LeTourneau, P.M., and Olsen, P.E., eds., The Great Rift Valleys of Pangea in Eastern North America (Volume 1): Columbia Univ. Press, New York, p. 80-103.

Marzoli, A., Jourdan, F., Puffer, J.H., Cuppone, T., Tanner, L.H., Weems, R.E., Bertrand, H., Cirilli, S., Bellieni, G. and De Min, A., 2011, Timing and duration of the Central Atlantic magmatic province in the Newark and Culpeper basins, eastern USA: Lithos, v. 122, no. 3, p.175-188.

McFarland, R.E., 2013, Sediment distribution and hydrologic conditions of the Potomac aquifer in Virginia and parts of Maryland and North Carolina: United States Geological Survey Scientific Investigations Report 2013-5116, p. 1-67.

Miller, H.W., 1967, Cretaceous vertebrates from Phoebus Landing, North Carolina: Proceedings of the Academy of Natural Sciences of Philadelphia, v. 119, no. 5, p. 219-235. [faunal list updated in Baird and Horner, 1979]

Miller, H.W., 1968, Additions to the Upper Cretaceous vertebrate fauna of Phoebus Landing, North Carolina. J. Elisha Mitchell Scientific Society, v. 84, no. 4, p.467-471. [faunal list updated in Baird and Horner, 1979]

National Park Service, 2013, Petrified Forest: Triassic dinosaurs and other animals, 2 p. (http://npshistory.com/brochures/pefo/triassic-animals-2013.pdf)

Ohno, S., Kadono, T., Kurosawa, K., Hamura, T., Sakaiya, T., Shigemori, K., Hironaka, Y., Sano, T., Watari, T., Otani, K. and Matsui, T.,

2014, Production of sulphate-rich vapour during the Chicxulub impact and implications for ocean acidification: Nature Geoscience, v. 7, no. 4, p.279.

Olsen, P. E., 1979, New aquatic eosuchian from the Newark Supergroup (Late Triassic-Early Jurassic) of North Carolina and Virginia: Postilla, v. 176, 14 p. [*Tanytrachelos*]

Olsen, P.E., and Baird, D., 1986, The ichnogenus *Atreipus* and its significance for Triassic Biostratigraphy *in* Padian, K. (ed.), The Beginning of the Age of Dinosaurs, Faunal Change Across the Triassic-Jurassic Boundary: New York, Cambridge University Press, p. 61-87.

Olsen, P. E., and Huber, P., 1997, Stop 3: Triangle Brick Quarry *in* Clark, T. W. (ed.), TRIBI: Triassic Basin Initiative, Abstracts with Programs and Field Trip Guidebook, Duke University, Durham, p. 22-29. [*Turseodus, Cionichthys, Semionotus, Pariostegus*]

Olsen, P.E., and Huber, P., 1998, The oldest Late Triassic footprint assemblage from North America (Pekin Formation, Deep River Basin, North Carolina, USA): Southeastern Geology, v. 38, no. 2, p. 77-90. [*Apatopus*, cf. *Atreipus, Brachychirotherium, Longosuchus, Placerias*]

Olsen, P.E., Kent, D.V., Sues, H.-D., Koeberl, C., Huber, H., Montanari, A., Rainforth, E.C., Fowell, S.J., Szajna, M.J., and Hartline, B.W., 2002, Ascent of dinosaurs linked to an iridium anomaly at the Triassic-Jurassic boundary: Science, v. 296, p. 1305-1307.

Olsen, P.E., and Johannson, S.K., 1994, Field guide to Late Triassic tetrapod sites in Virginia and North Carolina (Culpeper, Richmond, and Dan River basins, Newark Supergroup): in Sues, H.D., and Fraser, N. (eds.), In the Shadow of the Dinosaurs: Cambridge University Press, p. 408-430. [*Cionichthys, Dictyopyge, Lissodus, Tanaocrossus*]

Olsen, P.E., Reid, J.C., Taylor, K., Kent, D., Whiteside, J.H., 2015, Revised stratigraphy of Late Triassic age strata of the Dan River Basin (Virginia and North Carolina, USA) based on drill core and outcrop data: Southeastern Geology, v. 51, p. 1-31. [*Apatopus, Banisterobates, Brachychirotherium, Grallator, Synorichthys, Mecistotrachelos, Tanytrachelos*]

Olsen, P.E., Schlische, R.W., Gore, P.J.W., and others, 1989, Field Guide to the Tectonics, stratigraphy, sedimentology, and paleontology of the Newark Supergroup, eastern North America: International Geological Congress, Guidebooks for Field Trips T351, 174 p. [*Cionichthys, Dictyopyge, Semionotus, Synorichthys, Tanaocrossus, Turseodus,* cf. *Pariostegus, Osteopleurus* (=*Diplurus*), *Doswellia, Rutiodon, Atreipus, Grallator, Eubrontes*]

Osborn, H.F., 1886, A new mammal from the American Triassic: Science, v. 8, no. 201, p. 540. [*Microconodon*]

Parris, D.C., 1986, Biostratigraphy of the fossil crocodile *Hyposaurus* Owen from New Jersey: New Jersey State Museum, Publication no. 4, p.1-16.

Parris, D.C., Grandstaff, B.S., and Clements, D., 2004, A pterosaur femur from the Upper Cretaceous of North Carolina: Southeastern Geology, v. 43, no. 1, p. 51-55. [*Enchodus, Cimoliasaurus, Peritresius,* aff. *Azhdarcho*]

Parris, D.C., Grandstaff, B.S., and Gallagher, W.B., 2004, A lungfish (dipnoan) from the Upper Cretaceous of New Jersey: The Mosasaur, v. 7, p. 65-68. [*Ceratodus* aff. *C. frazieri*; here listed as late Campanian but Hajzer et al. (2018) revise this occurrence to early Maastrichtian]

Parris, D.C., Schein, J.P., Daeschler, E.B., Gilmore, E.S., Poole, J.C. and Pellegrini, R.A., 2014, Two halves make a holotype: two hundred years between discoveries: Proceedings of the Academy of Natural Sciences of Philadelphia, v. 163, no. 1, p.85-89. [*Atlantochelys*]

Paul, G.S., 2016, Princeton Field Guide to Dinosaurs: Princeton University Press, 2nd edition, 360 p.

Petersen, S.V., Dutton, A., and Lohmann, K.C., 2016, End-Cretaceous extinction in Antarctica linked to both Deccan volcanism and meteorite impact via climate change: Nature communications, v. 7, no. 1, p.1-9.

Peyer, K., Carter, J.G., Novak, S.E., Sues, H.-D., and Olsen, P.E., 2008, A new suchian archosaur from the Upper Triassic of North Carolina: Journal of Vertebrate Paleontology, v. 28, no. 2, p. 363-381. [*Postosuchus*]

Redfield, William C., 1841, Short notices of American fossil fishes: American Journal of Science and Art, vol. 41, p. 24-28. [*Dictyopyge*]

Reinhardt, J., Christopher, R.A., and Owens, J.P., 1980, Lower Cretaceous stratigraphy of the core: Geology of the Oak Grove core, Virginia Division of Mineral Resources Publication 20, p. 31-52.

Retallack, G.J., and Dilcher, D.L., 1986, Cretaceous angiosperm invasion of North America: Cretaceous Research, v. 7, p. 227-252.

Rizzo, C.A., 1999, Evidence for live birth in the Triassic Coelacanth *Diplurus (Osteopleurus) newarki*: The Mosasaur, v. 6, p. 91-95.

Robb, A.J., III, 1989, The Upper Cretaceous (Campanian, Black Creek Formation) fossil fish fauna of Phoebus Landing, Bladen County, North Carolina: The Mosasaur, v. 4, p. 75-92. [*Adocus, Albula, Anomoeodus, Bothremys, Brachychampsa* (= *Leidyosuchus*), *Brachyrhizodus, Cylindracanthus, Deinosuchus, Dryptosaurus, Enchodus, Halisaurus, Hybodus, Hypsibema, Ischyodus, Ischyrhyza,* Lepisosteidae indet., *Odontaspis, Ornithomimus, Paralbula, Platecarpus, Prognathodon, Rhombodus, Saurodon, Scapanorhyncus, Squalicorax, Squatina, Stephanodus, Synodontaspis, Taphrosphys, Thoracosaurus,* "*Trionyx*," *Tylosaurus, Xiphactinus*]

Rose, K.D., 2000, Land-mammals from the late Paleocene Aquia Formation: The first early Cenozoic mammals from Maryland: Proceedings of the Biological Society of Washington, v. 113, p. 855-863. [Arctocyanidae indet., *Ectoganus, Phenacodus*]

Rose, P.J., 2007, A new titanosauriform sauropod (Dinosauria: Saurischia) from the Early Cretaceous of central Texas and its phylogenetic relationships: Palaeontologia Electronica, v. 10, no. 2, art. 8A. [*Astrodon*]

Sachs, S., and Kear, B.P., 2015, Fossil Focus: Elasmosaurs: Palaeontology Online, v. 5, Art. 2, p. 1-8. [*Elasmosaurus*]

Schaeffer, B., and McDonald, N.G., 1978, Redfieldiid fishes from the Triassic-Liassic Newark Supergroup of eastern North America: American Museum of Natural History Bulletin 159, art. 4, p. 131-173. [*Dictyopyge, Redfieldius, Tanaocrossus*]

Schulte, P., Alegret, L., Arenillas, I., Arz, J.A., Barton, P.J., Bown, P.R., Bralower, T.J., Christeson, G.L, et al., 2010, The Chicxulub Asteroid Impact and Mass Extinction at the Cretaceous-Paleogene Boundary: Science, v. 327, no. 5970, p. 1214–1218.

Schwimmer D.R., 2002, King of the crocodylians: the Paleobiology of *Deinosuchus*: Indiana University Press, p. 1-220.

Schwimmer, D.R., Sanders, A.E., Erickson, B.R., and Weems, R.E., 2015, A Late Cretaceous dinosaur and reptile assemblage from South Carolina, USA : Transactions of the American Philosophical Society, v. 105, no. 2, p. 1-157. [*Adocus, Agomphus, Bothremys, Chedighaii, Corsochelys, Euclastes, Osteopygis, Peritresius, Prionochelys, Protostega, Saurornitholestes, Taphrosphys, "Trionyx"*]

Schwimmer, D.R., Stewart, J.D., and Williams, G.D., 1994, Giant fossil coelacanths of the Late Cretaceous in the eastern United States: Geology, v. 22, no. 6, p. 503-506. [*Megacoelacanthus*]

Shaler, N.S., and Woodworth, J.B., 1899, Geology of the Richmond basin, Virginia *in* Walcott, C. D., ed., Nineteenth annual report of the United States Geological Survey to the Secretary of the Interior, 1897–1898; Part II, Papers chiefly of a theoretic nature: United States Geological Survey Annual Report 19: p. 385–519.

Smith, A.G., Smith, D.G., and Funnell, B.M., 2004, Atlas of Mesozoic and Cenozoic Coastlines: Cambridge University Press, 99 p.

Spangler, W.B., 1950, Subsurface geology of Atlantic Coastal Plain in North Carolina: American Association of Petroleum Geologists, v. 34, no. 1, p. 100-132.

Stanford, R., Lockley, M.G., Tucker, C., Godfrey, S., and Stanford, S.M., 2018, A diverse mammal-dominated, footprint assemblage from wetland deposits in the Lower Cretaceous of Maryland: Scientific Reports, v. 8, p. 741 | DOI:10.1038/s41598-017-18619-w [*Aquatilavipes, cf. Pteraichnus, Sederipes, cf. Tetrapodosaurus*]

Stanford, R., Lockley, M.K., and Weems, R.E., 2007, Diverse dinosaur-dominated ichnofaunas from the Potomac Group (Lower Cretaceous), Maryland: Ichnos, v. 14, p. 155-173.

Stanford, R., Weems, R.E., and Lockley, M.K., 2004, A new dinosaur ichnotaxon from the Lower Cretaceous Patuxent Formation of Maryland and Virginia: Ichnos, v. 11, p. 251-259. [*Hypsiloichnus*]

Stanford, R., Weishampel, D.B., and DeLeon, D.B., 2011, The first hatchling dinosaur reported from the eastern United States: *Pro-*

planoplosaurus marylandicus (Dinosauria: Ankylosauria) from the Early Cretaceous of Maryland, USA: Journal of Paleontology, v. 85, no. 4, p. 916-924.

Stose, G.W., and Jonas, A.I., 1939, Geology and mineral resources of York County, Pennsylvania: Pennsylvania Geological Survey, 4th series, Bulletin C67, 199 p. [*Pentasauropus*]

Stringer, Gary, and Schwarzhans, Werner, 2021, Upper Cretaceous teleostean otoliths from the Severn Formation (Maastrichtian) of Maryland, USA, with an unusual occurrence of Siluriformes and Beryciformes and the oldest Atlantic Coast Gadiformes: Cretaceous Research, v. 125, p. 1-29. [*Albula, Ampheristis, Anguilla?, Apateodus, Argyroberyx?, Arius?, Congrophichthus, Cowetaichthys, Eutawichthys, Holocentronotus, Hoplopteryx, Hoplostethus, Ichthyotringa?, Kokenichthys, Muraenanguilla, Osmeroides, Ossulcus, Otolithopsis, Palaeogadus, Paraulopus, Pempheris?, Pterothrissus, Severnichthys, Vorhisia*]

Sues, H.-D., 1992, A Remarkable New Armored Archosaur from the Upper Triassic of Virginia: Journal of Vertebrate Paleontology, v. 12, no. 2, p. 142–149. [*Euscolosuchus*]

Sues, H.-D., 2001, On *Microconodon*, a Late Triassic cynodont from the Newark Supergroup of eastern North America: Bulletin of the Museum of Comparative Zoology, v. 156, no. 1, p. 37-48.

Sues, H.-D., and Olsen, P. E., 1993, A new procolophonid and a new tetrapod of uncertain, possibly procolophonian affinities from the Upper Triassic of Virginia: Journal of Vertebrate Paleontology, v. 13, no. 3, p. 282-286. [*Gomphiosauridion, Xenodiphiodon*]

Sues, H.-D., and Olsen, P.E., 2015, Stratigraphic and temporal context and faunal diversity of Permian-Jurassic continental tetrapod assemblages from the Fundy rift basin, eastern Canada: Atlantic Geology, v. 51, p. 139-205.

Sues, H.-D., and Olsen, P.E., 1999, A Late Triassic traversodont cynodont from the Newark Supergroup of North Carolina: Journal of Vertebrate Paleontology, v. 19, no. 2, p. 351-354. [*Boreogomphodon, Plinthogomphodon*]

Sues, H.-D., Olsen, P.E., and Carter, J.G., 2003, A new crocodylomorph archosaur from the Upper Triassic of North Carolina: Journal of Vertebrate Paleontology, v. 23, p. 329-343. [*Dromicosuchus*]

Sues, H.-D., Olsen, P.E. and Kroehler, P.A., 1994, Small tetrapods from the Upper Triassic of the Richmond basin (Newark Supergroup Virginia *in* N.C. Fraser and H.-D. Sues (eds.), In the Shadow of the Dinosaurs, Cambridge University Press, p. 161-170. [*Boreogomphodon, Microconodon, Uatchitodon,* Lepidosauria indet.]

Sues, H.-D., and Schoch, R.R., 2013, Anatomy and phylogenetic relationships of *Calamops paludosus* (Temnospondyli, Stereospondyli) from the Triassic of the Newark Basin, Pennsylvania: Journal of Vertebrate Paleontology, v. 33, no. 5, p. 1061-1070. doi:10.1080/02724634.2 013.759120.

Sulej, T., and Niedźwiedzki, G., 2019, An elephant-sized Late Triassic synapsid with erect limbs: Science. doi:10.1126/science.aal4853. ISSN 0036-8075

Upchurch, G.R., Crane, P.R., and Drinnan, A.N., 1994, The megaflora from the Quantico locality (Upper Albian), Lower Cretaceous Potomac Group of Virginia: Virginia Museum of Natural History Memoir 4, p. 1-57.

Vellekoop, J., Esmeray-Senlet, S., Miller, K.G., Browning, J.V., Sluijs, A., van de Schootbrugge, B., Damsté, J.S.S., and Brinkhuis, H., 2016, Evidence for Cretaceous-Paleogene boundary bolide "impact winter" conditions from New Jersey, USA: Geology, v. 44, no. 8, p. 619-622.

Weems, R.E., 1980a, An unusual newly discovered archosaur from the Upper Triassic of Virginia, U.S.A.: Transactions of the American Philosophical Society, v. 70, p. 1-53. [*Doswellia,* Phytosauridae, *Poposaurus*]

Weems, R.E., 1980b, Geology of the Taylorsville basin, Hanover County, Virginia *in* Contributions to Virginia geology – IV: Virginia Division of Mineral Resources Publication 27, p. 23–28.

Weems, R.E., 1987, A late Triassic footprint fauna from the Culpeper Basin, northern Virginia: Transactions of the American Philosophical Society, v. 77, no. 1, p. 1-79. [*Agrestipus* (= *Brachychirotherium*), *Anchisauripus, Apatichnus* (= *Kayentapus*), *Eubrontes* (= *Kayentapus*), *Grallator, Gregaripus* (= *Anomoepus*)]

Weems, R.E., 1998, Newly recognized en echelon fall lines in the Piedmont and Blue Ridge provinces of North Carolina and Virginia; with a discussion of their possible ages and origins: U.S. Geological Survey, Open-File Report 98-374, 40 p.

Weems, R.E., 2014, Paleogene chelonians from Maryland and Virginia: PaleoBios, v. 31, no. 1, p. 1-32. [*Adocus, Aspideretoides*, Bothremyinae indet., *Catapleura, Eosphargis, Euclastes, Judithemys*, Kinosternid B, *Lophochelys, Planetochelys, Tasbacka, "Trionyx"*]

Weems, R.E., 2018, A synopsis of the vertebrate fauna from the Culpeper Basin (Upper Triassic-Lower Jurassic, Maryland and Virginia) *in* Lucas, S.G. and Sullivan, R.M., eds., Fossil Record 6. New Mexico Museum of Natural History and Science Bulletin 79, p. 749-768. [*Anomoepus, Apatopus, Batrachopus, Brachychirotherium, Chirotherium, Cionichthys, Diplurus, Eubrontes, Grallator, Gwyneddichnium, Kayentapus, Plesiornis*, prosauropod exoliths, *Ptycholepis, Redfieldius, Rhynchosauroides. Semionotus, Tanaocrossus*]

Weems, R.E., 2019, Evidence for bipedal prosauropods as the likely *Eubrontes* track-makers: Ichnos, v. 26, no. 3, p. 187-215. [*Anchisaurus, Eubrontes*]

Weems, R.E., 2021a, Behavioral patterns of the Late Triassic *Kayentapus minor* trackmakers at the Culpeper Quarry near Stevensburg, Virginia, USA *in* Lucas, S. G., Hunt, A. P. & Lichtig, A. J., Fossil Record 7: New Mexico Museum of Natural History and Science Bulletin 82, p. 459-474. [*Kayentapus, Liliensternus*]

Weems, R.E., 2021b, Additions and a taxonomic update to the dinosaur ichnofauna from the Patuxent Formation in Virginia, USA *in* Lucas, S. G., Hunt, A. P. & Lichtig, A. J., Fossil Record 7: New Mexico Museum of Natural History and Science Bulletin 82, p. 475-485. [*Brontopodus, Caririchnium, Gypsichnites, Hadrosauropodus, Hypsiloichnus, Irenesauripus, Ornithomimus, Tetrapodosaurus, Tyrannosauripus*]

Weems, R.E., and Bachman, J.M., 1997, Cretaceous anuran and dinosaur footprints from the Patuxent Formation of Virginia: Proceedings of the Biological Society of Washington, v. 110, p. 1-17. [*Amblydactylus* (= *Caririchnium*), *Megalosauropus* (= *Tyrannosauripus*)]

Weems, R.E., and Bachman, J.M., 2015, The Lower Cretaceous Patuxent Formation ichnofauna of Virginia: Ichnos, v. 22, p. 208-219. [*Amblydactylus* (= *Caririchnium*), *Brontopodus*, *Caririchnium* (= *Hadrosauropodus*), *Emydhipus*, *Gypsichnites*, *Hypsiloichnus*, *Megalosauropus*, *Ornithomimipus*, *Paraelops*, *Tetrapodosaurus*]

Weems, R.E., and Lucas, S.G., 2015, A revision of the Norian conchostracan zonation in North America and its implication for Late Triassic North American tectonic history *in* Sullivan, R.M. and Lucas, S.G., eds., Fossil Record 4. New Mexico Museum of Natural History and Science Bulletin 67, p. 303–317.

Weems, R.E., Self-Trail, J.M., and Edwards, L.E., 2019, Cross section of the North Carolina coastal plain from Enfield through Cape Hatteras: U.S. Geological Survey, Open-File Report 2019–1145, 2 sheets, https://doi.org/10.3133/ofr20191145.

Weems, R.E., Tanner, L.H., and Lucas, S.G., 2016, Synthesis and revision of the litho-stratigraphic groups and formations in the Upper Permian?–Lower Jurassic Newark Supergroup of eastern North America: Stratigraphy, v. 13, no. 2, p. 111–153.

Weishampel, D.B., Dodson, P. and Osmólska, H. eds., 2008, The Dinosauria. University of California Press, 3rd edition, 861 p.

Zanno, L.E., Drymala, S., Nesbitt, S.J., and Schneider, V.P., 2015, Early crocodylomorph increases top tier predator diversity during rise of dinosaurs: Scientific Reports. 5: 9276. doi:10.1038/srep09276. PMC 4365386 Freely accessible. PMID 25787306 [*Carnufex*]

APPENDIX 1
SUPERSCRIPT NOTES FROM TEXT

Chapter 1

1. There is a thorough posting on this animal in Wikipedia. The formal description is at: Nesbitt, S.J.; Barrett, P.M.; Werning, S.; Sidor, C.A.; Charig, A.J., 2013, The oldest dinosaur? A Middle Triassic dinosauriform from Tanzania: Biology Letters, v. 9, 20120949. doi:10.1098/rsbl.2012.0949. PMC 3565515 Freely accessible. PMID 23221875.

2. There is a detailed summary of this event in Wikipedia. There is also abundant formal literature on this subject including: Benton, M.J., 2005, When life nearly died: The greatest mass extinction of all time: London, Thames & Hudson, ISBN 0-500-28573-X; Sahney, S., and Benton, M.J., 2008, Recovery from the most profound mass extinction of all time: Proceedings of the Royal Society B, v. 275, no. 1636, p. 759–765. doi:10.1098/rspb.2007.1370. PMC 2596898 Freely accessible. PMID 18198148.

3. Living birds are classified in their own feathered group (Class Aves), distinct from the other two primarily land-dwelling vertebrate groups classified as the scaly reptiles (Class Reptilia) and the furry and breast-bearing mammals (Class Mammalia). When these groups were first defined in the mid-1700s, the prehistoric animals known today as dinosaurs were neither recognized nor defined. It was not until 1842, when Richard Owen first coined the name "Dinosauria," that the scientific community began to appreciate that there once had existed a whole group of prehistoric animals

unlike anything living today. When the earliest discoveries of fragmentary dinosaur remains were announced, their discoverers concluded that they must have been some kind of prehistoric reptilian creatures. Soon after dinosaurs were defined, it became apparent that these creatures had one of three basic body plans, which became the basis for recognizing the major subgroups of dinosaurs: ornithischians, sauropods, and theropods (Figure 1). It wasn't until 1986 that a distinctive group within the theropod dinosaurs was defined and named maniraptorans, which had strikingly bird-like characteristics, including (at least in some cases) feathers. Since 1986, more and more species placed within this prehistoric group also have been shown to have had feathers, and it is now generally assumed that all maniraptorans were feathered. Yet despite this, they still remain classified among the theropod dinosaurs. This is in great measure an artifact of the history of dinosaur research. When the first maniraptorans were described in the late 1800s, they were not recognized to have had feathers, so they were classified as theropod dinosaurs, which they certainly did greatly resemble. If maniraptorans were reclassified as early bird cousins within the class Aves, because they have feathers and a number of other features in common with birds and not with dinosaurs, then by definition, maniraptorans would become excluded from the definition of dinosaurs. In that case, the end of the age of dinosaurs could be placed without argument at about 66 million years ago, when all non-maniraptoran dinosaurs abruptly died off.

4. For detailed summaries of conchostracan biostratigraphy in the Newark Supergroup, interested readers should consult Kozur and Weems (2010) for all but the Norian stage, which has been updated by Weems and Lucas (2015).

5. The correlation of Interstate 95 in Virginia with the western border of the Virginia Coastal Plain is not accidental. The western border

of the Virginia Coastal Plain is marked by a north-south trending fault zone that expresses itself in the modern landscape as the toe of a series of fall zones along each of the major rivers that empty into the Chesapeake Bay. These fall zones, when linked together along the fault zone that created them, form a geologic feature called the Tidewater Fall Line (Weems, 1998). Because each of these fall zones marked the head of maritime navigation up the major rivers of colonial Tidewater Virginia, towns and cities inevitably arose at the foot of each fall zone to unload and load commerce, including Georgetown in Washington, D.C., and Fredericksburg, Richmond, and Petersburg in Virginia. These major cities along the eastern edge of the Tidewater Fall Line were eventually linked by railroad and then later by the highways named U.S. Route 1 and Interstate 95. All three follow close to the trace of the Tidewater Fall Line.

Chapter 2

6. The details of this revised Newark Supergroup stratigraphic analysis and synthesis can be found in Weems et al. (2016).

7. Sir Charles Lyell was one of the Scottish pioneers of the geologic discipline of stratigraphy and the author of the book *Principles of Geology* (1830-33), in which he introduced, among other contributions to modern geologic thought, the concept of uniformitarianism. He defined and introduced a number of terms into geologic terminology that are still used today, including the major time divisions Paleozoic, Mesozoic, and Cenozoic. He wrote two books on his travels to America, *Travels in North America* (1845) and *A Second Visit to the United States* (1849). Both books provide very readable and worthwhile glimpses into the geology and human social life in the United States in the 1840s, including Virginia.

8. The best recent synopsis of the flora of the Richmond coal swamps

is to be found in Cornet and Olsen (1990). References to older paleobotanical literature can be found therein.

9. An excellent overview of the early Mesozoic faunachrons and the animals that characterize them is to be found in Lucas (2010).

10. Most of the geologic terms and the names of prehistoric animals used in this book are defined and discussed in Wikipedia. Because this source is so readily available in this day and age, it is here assumed that any names or terms unfamiliar to readers can be readily found there and that these terms therefore do not need to be defined separately in a glossary here.

11. Cornet and Olsen (1990).

12. Sues and Schoch (2013).

13. Sues and Olsen (1993).

14. Sues, Olsen, and Kroehler (1994).

15. Weems (1980a).

16. Sues (1992).

Chapter 3

17. Major Virginia references to petrified wood of *Araucarioxylon virginianum* are found in Shaler and Woodworth (1899) for the Richmond Basin, in Weems (1980b) for the Taylorsville Basin, and in Olsen et al. (2015) and references cited therein for the Danville/Dan River Basin. A recent paper on *Araucarioxylon arizonicum* (Ash and Creber, 2000) is available online at https://onlinelibrary.wiley.com/doi/pdf/10.1111/1475-4983.00116; it shows a restoration of the likely appearance of this tree in life.

18. Olsen and Huber (1998).

19. Fraser et al. (1996).

20. Lucas and Tanner (2018a).

21. The other major coal producing region in the Newark Supergroup was in the Deep River basins in North Carolina, where upper Car-

nian coals were mined from the Cumnock Member of the Lockatong Formation. A summary of the history of this industry and the geology of these coal beds can be found in Campbell and Kimball (1923).

22. Schaeffer and MacDonald (1978).
23. Olsen and Huber (1997) and Olsen et al. (1989).
24. Heckert et al. (2012).
25. Leidy (1856), updated in Colbert and Imbrie (1956).
26. Fraser et al. (2007).
27. Olsen (1979).
28. Bock (1945), revised in Huene (1948).
29. Peyer et al. (2008).
30. Cope (1871).
31. Emmons (1856, 1860); Olsen et al. (1989).
32. Heckert et al. (2015).
33. Zanno et al. (2015).
34. Sues, Olsen, and Carter (2003).
35. Olsen and Baird (1986); Fraser and Olsen (1996); Olsen et al. (2015).
36. Sues and Olsen, 1999; Liu, Schneider, and Olsen (2017).
37. Osborn (1886); Sues (2001); Heckert et al. (2012).
38. Olsen and Huber (1998); Green et al. (2005).

Chapter 4

39. Well documented reports on the geology and stratigraphy of the Culpeper Basin are given in Lindholm (1979) and Lee and Froelich (1989). Paleoclimate of the basin is discussed in Gore and Traverse (1986). The most recent update for the stratigraphy of Culpeper Basin is in Weems et al. (2016). Details of the types of vertebrate remains in the Culpeper Basin and their stratigraphic ranges are summarized in Weems (2018).

40. Climates similar to those in Virginia during the Norian exist today in the Basin and Range region of the western United States. In parts of that region, rift valleys are filling that have environments very similar to Virginia during much of the Norian stage, including alluvial fans along fault-bounded margins of the valleys, dry brush-covered playa flats, and ephemeral to persistent alkaline (or soda) lakes hostile to most forms of fresh-water life including fish. A visit to this region is in many ways a visit back to Virginia 210 million years ago.

41. A more detailed description of the vertebrate fossils known from the Culpeper Basin and the earlier literature on them can be found in Weems (2018). There is a new paper analyzing in detail the behavior of the *Kayentapus minor* trackmakers at the Culpeper Quarry (Weems, 2021a).

42. This discovery is documented in LeTourneau (2003).

43. The Norian dicynodont tracks from southern Pennsylvania are discussed in Key and Delano (1993) and illustrated in Stose and Jonas (1939). The Polish Norian dicynodont skeleton is described in Sulej and Niedźwiedzki (2019).

44. An informative discussion of Revueltian and other Triassic faunas from a global perspective can be found in Lucas (1998).

Chapter 5

45. The evidence for this, primarily from the Taylorsville Basin, is given in Malinconico (2003).

46. The region where rocks formed during this major volcanic event is known as the Central Atlantic Magmatic Province (CAMP). The volcanic rocks that formed in this region, now dispersed by the formation and spread of the Atlantic Ocean Basin, are found today from Bolivia through eastern North America and Morocco, to westernmost Europe and Greenland. A good introduction to these

rocks from an eastern North American perspective can be found in Marzoli et al. (2011).

47. The evidence for a short duration of deposition for the Partridge Island Member is discussed in Olsen et al. (2002).

48. Recognition of this uppermost Rhaetian interval in the Culpeper Basin is documented in Weems et al. (2016) and references therein to related previous work.

49. Lucas and Tanner (2018b).

Chapter 6

50. The most up-to-date summary of the Early Jurassic fauna in the Culpeper Basin is in Weems (2018). Earlier work is summarized and references for this earlier work are provided.

51. The case for *Eubrontes* representing the tracks of a prosauropod dinosaur is presented in Weems (2019).

52. Very nice pictures of some of the small Wassonian vertebrates found in the Fundy Basin in Canada can be seen in Sues and Olsen (2015), which is available online. The stratigraphy used in this paper has been updated in Weems et al. (2016).

Chapter 7

53. Stratigraphy of a deep well and associated cores taken offshore of Newfoundland is described in Cousminer and Steinkraus (1988); the stratigraphy of the deep well and associated cores taken at Cape Hatteras is described in Spangler (1950) and in Weems et al. (2019).

54. For readers interested in learning more about the Morrison Formation dinosaurs, a good place to start is Foster (2007). It is well worth a visit to see some of these dinosaurs where they were found at Dinosaur National Monument, Utah.

55. The most current summary of this fauna is by Iturralde-Vinent and Izquierdo (2015), which can be accessed online.

Chapter 8

56.   The most recent regional work on the Potomac Group in Virginia, where it is essentially synonymous with the Potomac Aquifer, was published by McFarland (2013). This includes much information on the subsurface distribution of this group throughout the Coastal Plain region of Virginia. For fossil and outcrop information, the classic work on the Cretaceous of Virginia remains Clark et al. (1912), though the taxonomy used there is quite out of date.

57.   The most recent and very informative report on the paleobotany of the Patapsco Formation in northern Virginia is by Upchurch et al. (1994). For the Dutch Gap site on the James River, the classic work by Clark et al. (1912) remains the principal reference.

58.   The stratigraphic relationships of the Arundel Formation remain uncertain. The Arundel could represent a series of valley-fill deposits that formed on the eroded upper surface of the Patuxent Formation, then were subsequently erosionally planed off, isolated, and covered by deposits of the overlying Patapsco Formation. Alternatively, the Arundel could consist of slack-water channel-fill deposits that formed while the upper part of the Patuxent Formation was forming. If the former case proves true, the Arundel should remain a separate formational unit. If the latter case proves true, it should be reduced to member status within the Patuxent Formation. There is no evidence for the Arundel in Virginia.

59.   This Patuxent climate discussion is considered in greater detail in Weems and Bachman (2015).

60.   The occurrence of glauconite in the Oak Grove core is documented in Reinhardt et al. (1980).

61.   The structure contour map on the base of the Potomac aquifer in McFarland (2013, Figure 6) clearly shows the strong northeastward shift in trend of the Potomac Group north of Fredericksburg

and the very rapid northwestward thinning of that unit, which reflects northwest-side uplift along the Stafford fault system that caused the inland facies of the Patuxent to be removed, probably prior to the late Paleocene. In the Early Cretaceous, the fault line that demarked the western edge of the Patuxent Group continued almost due north beyond Washington, D.C., before the edge of the Coastal Plain shifted eastward in Maryland.

62. Clark et al. (1912) is still the main source for information on the complexion of the Patuxent megaflora in Virginia. Berry (1911a) provides the most comprehensive overview of the Patuxent and Patapsco floras in Maryland. A more recent analysis of the Cretaceous floras of this region is found in Retallack and Dilcher (1986). Discussions of pollen from the Patuxent are in Doyle and Hickey (1976) and in Doyle and Robbins (1977). Weems et al. (2019) document the marine fossil evidence for correlating the Patuxent with the early Albian, rather than the late Aptian as argued in earlier papers.

63. Megaflora from the Patapsco Formation in Virginia is described in Upchurch et al. (1994). The palynoflora of the Patapsco is discussed in Doyle and Hickey (1976) and in Doyle and Robbins (1977).

64. Weems and Bachman (2015).

65. Kranz (1998) and Frederickson et al. (2016).

66. The frog tracks are reported in Weems and Bachman (1997); the turtle tracks are reported in Weems and Bachman (2015).

67. Lipka et al. (2006) describe *Arundelemys*; *Glyptops* and *Naomichelys* are listed in Kranz (1998). All are summarized in Frederickson et al. (2018).

68. Frederickson et al. (2018).

69. Lockley et al. (2008).

70. The name *Astrodon* was coined by Christopher Johnston in 1859

for sauropod teeth found in the Arundel Formation with star-shaped patterns in the cross-section of their roots. Johnston did not designate a species name to go with his generic name *Astrodon* when he named it, so Joseph Leidy added the species name *johnstoni* in 1865, which he designated in honor of Christopher Johnston's earlier work. In 1888, Othniel Marsh described other sauropod skeletal remains from the Arundel Formation under the names *Pleurocoelous nanus* and *P. altus* in the belief that they belonged to a sauropod that was different from *A. johnstoni*. Later workers have generally agreed that all of these names only describe different growth stages of a single sauropod species, and *Astrodon johnstoni* is the oldest name applicable to this material (Carpenter and Tidwell, 2005). However, Rose (2007) has argued that the type tooth material of *Astrodon* is not really diagnostic, and because the type material of *Pleurocoelous* is somewhat more complete, the name *Pleurocoelous* should be given priority over the name *Astrodon*. Others, such as d'Emic (2013), argue that neither genus is based on truly diagnostic material. Until better material of *A. johnstoni* is found in the Arundel, the diagnosis of this taxon necessarily will remain incomplete and less than definitive. In the meantime, for our purposes, the oldest properly applied name is the one used here.

71. Weems and Bachman (2015).

72. *Diplodocus* is estimated to have reached a length of 82 feet (Paul, 2016), while *Brachiosaurus* is estimated to have reached a length of 85 feet (Holtz, 2008). *Supersaurus* has been estimated to reach an astounding 110 feet in length (Lovelace et al., 2007).

73. Carpenter and Tidwell (2005).

74. Stanford et al. (2004).

75. Weems and Bachman (2015); Weems (2021b).

76. Stanford et al. (2011).

77. Chinnery et al. (1998).
78. Harris (1998); Lipka (1998).
79. Weems and Bachman (1997); Weems (2021b).
80. Weems (2021b).
81. The raptors portrayed in the *Jurassic Park* and *Jurassic World* films were similar in appearance to the species of *Deinonychus* that lived here in the Early Cretaceous, but very much larger. Even so, the behavior of the raptors portrayed in these films is still useful for envisioning the likely behavior of the smaller Early Cretaceous *Deinonychus* that lived in our region.
82. Lipka (1998).
83. Brownstein (2017); Frederickson et al. (2018).

Chapter 9

84. The most comprehensive documentation of this relationship is still Clark et al. (1912).
85. The name Appalachia has been in use for the eastern American mid-Cretaceous to Late Cretaceous island continent at least since Schwimmer (2002). The term was used much earlier for a hypothetical continent that was supposed to have existed off the coast of eastern North America in the Paleozoic, from which sediment was shed into the ancient Appalachian seaway from the east. The existence of such a continent has been disproven. Once plate tectonics became accepted, the hypothetical Paleozoic continent of Appalachia was realized to be Africa. Once that usage was debunked, the term Appalachia became available for the demonstrable Late Cretaceous island continent in eastern North America.
86. For more information on all of these geologic units, go to the U.S. Geological Survey Geolex Website (https://ngmdb.usgs.gov/Geolex/search). Type in the name of a unit, and a brief summary of it will appear along with links to major references and summaries

of their content. All of these strata fall within the Ancora Super-group except for the basal Elk Neck beds, which are part of the Marquesas Supergroup.

87. The palynoflora of the Virginia region during the Cenomanian is discussed in Doyle and Hickey (1976), Doyle and Robbins (1977), and Hansen (1992). Macroscopic plant remains are figured and discussed in Berry (1911b, 1916) and in Retallack and Dilcher (1986).

88. This site is described in Stanford et al. (2018). This locality was re-ported as belonging to the Lower Cretaceous Patuxent Formation, but it lies distinctly east of the Patuxent outcrop belt and within the outcrop belt of a unit at the very top of the Potomac Group once called the "Raritan Formation" (Clark, 1916), and more recently recognized as a unit somewhat older than the type Raritan in New Jersey and now known informally as the lower Cenomanian Elk Neck beds at the top of the Patapsco Formation (Hansen, 1992; Hansen and Drummond, 1994).

89. Stanford et al. (2018) suggested that one large track at this site belonged to a sauropod (their cf. *Brontopodus* sp.) but this seems unlikely. The track is rather unlike other *Brontopodus* tracks from the Early Cretaceous of Maryland and Virginia and instead ap-pears to be much more similar to manus tracks of *Tetrapodosau-rus*. By the time these tracks formed, the sauropod hiatus in North America was well underway (d'Emic and Foreman, 2012) and no definitive sauropod remains are known from anywhere in North America during the Cenomanian time interval. For both of these reasons, the large manus track from this site likely belongs to the same kind of animal as the pes track (cf. *Tetrapodosaurus* sp.) from this site. The small tracks called cf. *Grallator* sp. by Stanford et al. (2018) are more likely to represent the Cenomanian avian ichno-genus *Aquatilavipes* than the Early Cretaceous and older coeluro-

saurian ichnogenus *Grallator*. Even without the alleged sauropod track, this locality still represents by far the most diverse trackway assemblage known from the Cenomanian stage anywhere in eastern North America.

90. This metatarsal specimen was described by Baird (1989), who thought that this specimen, though not certainly identifiable, showed considerable resemblance to *Appalachiosaurus* (known in 1989 but not yet described). If there should prove to be a close connection between this metatarsal and *Appalachiosaurus,* it belonged to a tyrannosaurid.

Chapter 10

91. Information on Campanian bony fish is found in Baird and Horner (1979), Crane (2011), Gallagher et al. (1986), Garcia and Hippensteel (2011), Hartstein and Decina (1986), Hartstein et al. (1999), Huddleston and Savoie (1983), Lauginiger (1984), Miller (1967, 1968), Parris et al. (2004), Robb (1989), and Schwimmer et al. (1994).

92. Information on cartilaginous fish including sharks and rays is found in Baird and Horner (1979), Case (1979), Case et al. (2017), Crane (2011), Gallagher et al. (1986), Garcia and Hippensteel (2011), Hartstein and Decina (1986), Hartstein and Lauginiger (1983), Lauginiger (1984), Miller, (1967, 1968), and Robb (1989).

93. Information on Campanian sea turtles can be found in Parris et al. (2004, 2014) and in Schwimmer et al. (2015). The story of *Atlantochelys* is quite fascinating. It is based on the anterior end of a humerus that was described and published as the holotype of *Atlantochelys mortoni* in 1849. Until recently, this was all we knew about this taxon. Then Parris et al. (2014) reported the discovery of the distal lower half of this same humerus, which was found in the same area as the holotype and fits snuggly onto it. The two halves

of this humerus were finally reunited after being separated for more than 160 years!

94. Information on the Campanian elasmosaurid plesiosaur is found in Crane (2011).

95. Information on Campanian mosasaurs is found in Baird and Horner (1979), Crane (2011), Gallagher et al. (1986), Lauginiger (1984), and Robb (1989).

96. For information on *Thoracosaurus* in the Campanian see Baird and Galton (1981) and Robb (1989).

97. Iturralde-Vinent and Izquierdo (2015) recognize at least two kinds of ichthyosaurs from the Upper Jurassic of Cuba, so ichthyosaurs were almost certainly in the coastal waters of Virginia during the Late Jurassic and probably during the Early Cretaceous as well.

98. The most up-to-date information on the dinosaurs of Appalachia is found in Brownstein (2018a). References to older literature can be found therein.

99. See Denton and O'Neal (1995, 2008) for a detailed discussion; these lizards all come from the Ellisdale Fossil Site in New Jersey, which has a Wikipedia entry.

100. For New Jersey Campanian mammals, see Denton and O'Neill (2010), Grandstaff et al. (1992), and also the Ellisdale Fossil Site website; for the North Carolina mammal, see Crane (2011).

101. The report of *Pteranodon* is in Baird and Galton (1981). Harrell et al. (2016) reported *Arambourgiania* from western Tennessee.

102. Information on Campanian freshwater crocodilians is found in Baird and Galton (1981), Baird and Horner (1979), Crane (2011), Gallagher et al. (1986), Lauginiger (1984), and Robb (1989).

103. Information on Campanian freshwater turtles is found in Baird and Galton (1981), Crane (2011), Gallagher et al. (1986), Lauginiger (1984), Robb (1989), and Schwimmer et al. (2015).

104. Information on Campanian salamanders and frogs in New Jersey

is found in Denton and O'Neill (1998) and also see the "Ellisdale Fossil Site" at its Wikipedia webpage; for North Carolina, see Crane (2011).

105. Information on Campanian freshwater bony fishes is found in Crane (2011), Frederickson et al. (2016), Lauginiger (1984), and Robb (1989).

106. These Late Cretaceous dinosaurian faunal realms and their contrasts are discussed in Weishampel et al. (2008).

Chapter 11

107. Gallagher (1993).

108. Farke and Phillips (2017).

109. Brownstein (2018a and 2018b).

110. Krause and Baird (1979).

111. Parris et al. (2004) reported the *Azhdarcho* sp. femur from the Maastrichtian of North Carolina. Gallagher (1993) reported remains of a large Maastrichtian pterosaur under the name *Titanopteryx*. This name has proven to be preoccupied and so has been replaced by the name *Arambourgiania*. Harrell et al. (2016) have described a neck vertebra of *Arambourgiania philadelphiae* from western Tennessee which further confirms the presence of this pterosaur in eastern North America near the end of the Late Cretaceous.

112. Gallagher (1993).

113. Clarke J.A., Tambussi, C.P., Noriega J.I., Erickson G.M. and Ketcham R.A., 2005, Definitive fossil evidence for the extant avian radiation in the Cretaceous: Nature, v. 433, no. 7023, p.305-308.

114. Gallagher (1993), Gallagher et al. (1986), Garcia and Hippensteel (2011), Hartstein et al. (1999), and Schwimmer et al. (2015).

115. Hartstein et al. (1999), Gallagher (1993), Gallagher et al. (1986).

116. Garcia and Hippensteel (2011), Hartstein et al. (1999).

117. Information on the Maastrichtian lungfish tooth plates is found in

Parris et al. (2004) and in Hajzer et al. (2018).

118. Case (1979); Case et al. (2017), Gallagher (1993), Gallagher et al. (1986), Garcia and Hippensteel (2011), Hartstein and Decina (1986), Hartstein and Lauginiger (1983), Hartstein et al. (1999), and Parris et al. (2004).

119. Garcia and Hippensteel (2011), Hartstein and Decina (1986), Hartstein et al. (1999), Huddlestun and Savoie (1983), and Stringer and Schwarzhans (2021).

120. Gallagher (1993), Gallagher et al. (1986), Parris et al. (2004), Schwimmer et al. (2015).

121. Gallagher (1993), Gallagher et al. (1986), Parris et al. (2004).

122. Gallagher (1993), Gallagher et al. (1986).

123. Gallagher (1993), Gallagher et al. (1986), Holmes and Sues (2000).

124. Petersen et al. (2016) have the most recent and detailed account of these events. Their study was done on data derived from an expanded marine section sampled on Seymour Island in Antarctica.

125. Schulte et al. (2010).

126. Ohno et al. (2014).

127. Vellekoop et al. (2016).

128. This site is the first site discussed and illustrated in Dickas (2018).

129. Weems (2014) for turtles; Rose (2000) for land mammals.

APPENDIX 2
SOURCE CREDITS FOR FIGURES

1. Figure created by author.

2. Figure created by author.

3. Figure created by author.

4. Figure adapted by author from Smith et al. (2004).

5. *Dictyopyge macrura* adapted from Kahless28 at Deviant Art; *Lissodus* sp. is by F. Spindler and adapted from Fischer (2012); other fish images created by author.

6. *Leptopleuron* image adapted from "Leptopleuron lacertinum.jpg" by Nobu Tamura (2008) via Wikimedia Commons licensed under CC BY-SA 3.0; *Probelesodon* image adapted from "Probelesodon.jpg" by Smokeybjb (2009) via Wikimedia Commons licensed under CC BY-SA 3.0; *Erpetosuchus* image adapted from "Erpetosuchus BW white background.jpg by Nobu Tamura (2007) via Wikimedia Commons licensed under CC BY-SA 3.0; *Exaeretodon* image adapted from *The Cambridge Encyclopedia of Life Sciences*, ed. Adrian Friday & David S. Ingram, © Cambridge University Press 1985.

7. *Trematosaurus* and *Parasuchus* images adapted from Wikimedia Commons; *Doswellia kaltenbachi* from Weems (1980); *Poposaurus* image adapted from Wikipedia *Poposaurus* entry, restoration by Dr. Jeff Martz, National Park Service (2012).

8. Figures created by author except for *Arganodus* sp., which is adapted from Wikipedia *Arganodus* entry, restoration by Dr. Jeff Martz, National Park Service (2013); *Diplurus newarki* adapted from Fenton and Fenton (1958).

9. *Koskinonodon* adapted from "Metoposaurus diagnosticus kraselovi 1DB. jpg" by Dmitry Bogdanov (2007) via Wikimedia Commons licensed under CC BY-SA 3.0; *Gwyneddosaurus* adapted from "Tanytrachelos.jpg" via Prehistória Fandom licensed under CC BY-SA 3.0;

Mecistotrachelos adapted from Karen Carr (ralph@karencarr.com); *Brachyrhinodon* image adapted from "Brachyrhinodon BW.jpg" by Nobu Tamura (2008) via Wikimedia Commons licensed under CC BY-SA 3.0; *Revueltosaurus* image by Kahless28 on DeviantArt; *Banisterobates* prints taken from http://projectos.cienciaviva.pt/pw011/jazidas/banisterobates.holotipo.fraser.grimaldi.1997.jpg

10. *Placerias* image adapted from "Placerias1DB.jpg" byDmitry Bogdanov (2007) via Wikimedia Commons licensed under CC BY-SA 3.0; *Postosuchus* image adapted from "Postosuchus kirkpatricki.jpg" by Dr. Jeff Martz, National Park Service (2012) via Wikimedia Commons; *Gorgetosuchus* image adapted from Matt Celeskey via https://theappalachianonline.com/wp-content/uploads/2016/09/Gorgetosuchus_web_courtesy.jpg; *Carnufex* image adapted from "Carnufex carolinensis feeding on a dicynodont near a river bed" by Christopher DiPiazza (2015) via prehistoricbeastoftheweek.blogspot.com; *Rutiodon* image adapted from "Rutiodon BW.jpg" by Nobu Tamura (2007) via Wikimedia Commons licensed under CC BY-SA 3.0.

11. Figures adapted from Weems (2018) except *Diplurus newarki* which is from Fenton and Fenton (1958).

12. Figure from Weems (2018).

13. *Liliensternus* image adapted from Dinosaur Pictures and Facts; *Lisowicia* image adapted from "Dicynodont from PolandDB.jpg" by Dmitry Bogdanov (2008) via Wikimedia Commons licensed under CC BY-SA 3.0; *Coelophysis* image adapted from https://www.livingpaintings.org/wp-content/uploads/Coelophysis.jpg; *Heterodontosaurus* image adapted from nhm.ac.uk © The Trustees of the Natural History Museum, London, Licensed under the Open Government License; *Plateosaurus* image adapted from Dinosaurs 017, Orbis Play and Learn Collection via-read.ukprintarchive.com; *Redondasaurus* image adapted from "Redondasaurus" by Kahless28 (2009) via kahless28.deviantart.com; *Aetosaurus* image from Baird (1986); *Typothorax* image adapted from Matt Celeskey via https://www.newswise.com/articles/new-skeletons-from-the-age-of-dinosaurs-answere-century-old -questions.

14. Figure from Weems (2018).

15. Figure from Weems (2018).

16. *Coelophysis* image adapted from https://www.livingpaintings.org/ wp-content/uploads/Coelophysis.jpg; *Heterodontosaurus* image adapted from nhm.ac.uk © The Trustees of the Natural History Museum, London, Licensed under the Open Government License; *Dilophosaurus* image adapted from Sergey Krasovskiy; *Anchisaurus* adapted from *The Big Noisy Book of Dinosaurs* © Dorling Kindersley Limited; *Protosuchus* image adapted from Gabriel Ugueto via gabrielugueto.com.

17. Figure adapted by author from Smith et al. (2004).

18. *Camarasaurus* image adapted from Mineo Shiraishi; *Stegosaurus* image adapted from https://www.livingpaintings.org/wp-content/uploads/ Stegosaurus.jpg; *Allosaurus* image adapted from National Park Service (2019), no claim to original U.S. Government work; *Brachiosaurus* image adapted from Camus Altamirano via http://images. dinosaurpictures.org/brachiosaurus_altithorax_by_camusaltamirano-d4zvth3_89bf.jpg

19. *Rhamphorhynchus* adapted from Fenton and Fenton (1958); *Suchodus* image from "Suchodus durobrivense.jpg" by Dmitry Bogdanov, (2008) via Wikimedia Commons licensed under CC BY-SA 3.0; *Vinealesaurus* image adapted from "Vinialesaurus line-art" by Christopher Chávez (2012) via christopher252.deviantart.com; *Ophthalmosaurus* image adapted from "Ophthalmosaurus BW.jpg" by Nobu Tamura (2007) via Wikimedia Commons licensed under CC BY-SA 3.0.

20. Adapted from Dr. Ron Blakey website at http://jan.ucc.nau.edu/~rcb7/.

21. *Ceratodus* and *Hybodus images* are adapted from Fenton and Fenton (1958); *Lepidotes* is by Darren Pepper via www.prehistoric-wildlife. com; *Paraelops* image adapted from Fine Fossils (http://www.finefossils.com/products/Paraelops%20cearensis.htm); *Bernissartia* image by Nobu Tamura aka Arthur Weasly (2008) via Wikimedia Commons licensed under CC BY-SA 3.0; *Pholidosaurus* image adapted from Nobu Tamura (2012); *Goniopholis* by Biarmosuchus (https:// www.deviantart.com/biarmosuchus/gallery).

22. Figure created by author.

23. Image of *Deinonychus* from Emily Willoughby (e.deinonychus@gmail.com, emilywilloughby.com); *Aquilops* image adapted from "Aquilops NT small.jpg" by Nobu Tamura (2016) via Wikimedia Commons licensed under CCBY-SA 4.0; *Eotyrranus* image adapted from http://www.dinosaurisle.com/images/Eotyrannus-fleshed.jpg; *Zephyrosaurus* image adapted from http://alchetron.com/Zephyrosaurus; *Archaeornithomimus* image adapted from nhm.ac.uk © The Trustees of the Natural History Museum, London. Licensed under the Open Government License; *Triconodon* image adapted from http://image.wikifoundry.com/image/1/3rRMvhNyXysGxQ3KGXWqLA13555.

24. *Anhanguera* image adapted from "Anhanguera blittersdorffi" by Nobu Tamura (2009); *Tenontosaurus* image adapted from http://images.dinosaurpictures.org/tenontosaurus4_5dca.jpg; *Propanoplosaurus* image adapted from "Edmontonia dinosaur.png" by Mariana Ruiz (2006) via Wikimedia Commons licensed under public domain; *Eolambia* image adapted from https://www.jurassic-world.com/eolambia; *Acrocanthosaurus* image adapted from Sergey Krasovskiy; *Astrodon* image adapted from "Astrodon johnstoni.jpg" by Dmitry Bogdanov (2008) via Wikimedia Commons licensed under CC BY 3.0.

25. Geologic correlation chart created by author.

26. Map adapted from "North America 75 mya.png" by Ron Blakely, Colorado Plateau Geostystems (2012) via Wikimedia Commons licensed under CC BY 1.0.

27. Images adapted from Stanford et al. (2018), except *Irenesauripus* which is from Baird (1989).

28. *Albula* image adapted from http://www.floridasportsman.com/bone-fishb-4; *Anomoeodus* image from https://i0.wp.com/www.cretaceous-mantua.com/wp-content/uploads/2014/12/anomaeodus-phaseolus.png?resize=290%2C265&ssl=1; *Enchodus* image adapted from Darren Pepper via www.prehistoric-wildlife.com/; *Megalocoelacanthus* adapted from Schwimmer et al. (1994); *Xiphactinus* adapted from "Ichthyodectidae1.jpg" by Dmitry Bogdanov (2008) via Wikimedia Commons licensed under CC BY 3.0.

29. *Thoracosaurus* image adapted from "Thoracosaurus – Saurian" by Jacob Baardse via littlebaardo.arstation.com; *Protostega* image adapted from "Protostega gigas.jpg" by Dmitry Bogdanov (2008) via Wikimedia Commons licensed under CC BY 3.0,; *Globidens* image adapted from "GlobidensDB2.jpg" by Dmitry Bogdanov (2000) via Wikimedia Commons licensed under CC BY-SA 3; *Halisaurus* image adapted from http://www.bbc.co.uk/staticarchive/99cadcc642df982e02f-b038ac92fa60b53c6b903.jpg; *Platycarpus* image adapted from "Plate-carpus tympaniticus.jpg" by Dmitry Bogdanov (2010) via Wikimedia Commons licensed under CC BY 3.0; *Prognathodon* image adapted from "Prognath waipar2DB.jpg" by Dmitry Bogdanov (2008) via Wikimedia Commons licensed under CC BY 3.

30. *Appalachiosaurus* image adapted from "Appalachiosaurus montgome-riensis flipped.jpg" by FunkMonk (Michael B. H.) (2008) via Wiki-media Commons licensed under CC BY 3.0; *Dryptosaurus* adapted from "Dryptosaurus aquilunguis" by Robinson K. (2012) via tera-tophoneus.deviantart.com; *Lophorhothon* adapted from nhm.ac.uk © Anness Publishing / NHMPL; *Hadrosaurus* adapted from https://dino.wikia.org/wiki/Hadrosaurus.

31. *Pteranodon* adapted from Fenton and Fenton (1958); *Saurornitholestes* image adapted from https://dinopedia.fandom.com/wiki/Saurorni-tholestes; *Montanoceratops* image adapted from "Montanoceratops BW.jpg" by Nobu Tamura (2007) via Wikimedia Commons licensed under CC BY 3.0; *Ornithomimus* image adapted from Mineo Shirai-shi; *Panoplosaurus* image adapted from https://jurassicpark.fandom.com/wiki/Panoplosaurus.

32. *Albanerpeton* image adapted from "Albanerpeton BW.jpg" by Nobu Tamura (2007) via Wikimedia Commons licensed under CC BY 3.0; *Discoglossus* image adapted from https://imgc.allpostersimages.com/img/print/u-g-PINDIO0.jpg; *Coniophis* image adapted from https://i.pinimg.com/originals/8e/f1/7c/8ef17cb9eca004d5fe3d-4cea516e1e91.jpg; *Didelphodon* image adapted from "Didelphodon NT small.jpg" by Nobu Tamura (2016) via Wikimedia Commons licensed under CC BY-SA 4.0; *Gypsonichtops* adapted from Nix Il-lustration via alphynix.tumblr.com; *Mesodma* image adapted from https://dinopedia.fandom.com/wiki/Mesodma; *Apalone* image adapt-

ed from The Animal Diversity Web (online) via animaldiversity.org; *Podocnemis* image adapted from Joel Sartore via joelsartore.com; *Haptosphenus* image adapted from https//dinopedia.fandom.com/wiki/Haptosphenus.

33. *Brachychampsa* image adapted from "Brachychampsa NT small.jpg" by Nobu Tamura (2016) via Wikimedia Commons licensed under CC BY-SA 4.0; *Borealosuchus* image adapted from "Allodaposuchus BW.jpg" by Nobu Tamura (2007) via Wikimedia Commons licensed under CC BY 3.0; *Deinosuchus* image adapted from "Deinosuchus illustration Andrey Atuchin.jpg" by Andrey Atuchin (2014) via Wikimedia Commons licensed under CC BY-SA 4.0.

34. *Ceratodus* image adapted from Fenton and Fenton (1958); *Amia* image adapted from "Amia calva.jpg" by Edgar R. Waite (1901) via Wikimedia Commons licensed under public domain; *Atractosteus* image by Joseph Tomelleri, adapted from http://www.fishesoftexas.org/media/attachments/taxa/images/web/4508.jpg; *Acipenser* image adapted from Duane Raver/U.S. Fish and Wildlife Service - fws.gov.

35. Paleogeography adapted from figshare; impact effects adapted from the Lunar and Planetary Institute Chicxulub Impact Event website at www.lpi.usra.edu/science/kring/Chicxulub/regional-effects/. Location of the Chicxulub impact crater is indicated by star. Inner circle marks limit of total forest flattening; outer circle marks limit of gale to hurricane force winds as estimated on the Lunar and Planetary Institute Chicxulub Impact Event website. Note that the Western Interior Seaway has become greatly reduced by this time.

36. *Arambourgiania* image adapted from John Sibbick via http://images.dinosaurpictures.org/Arambourgiania_0402.jpg; *Azhdarcho* image adapted from Fabrizio De Rossi via https://www.pteros.com/pterosaurs/azhdarcho.html; *Hypacrosaurus* image adapted from "Hypacrosaurus altispinus" by Pachyornis (2013) via pachyornis.deviantart.com; *Triceratops* image adapted from Fenton and Fenton (1958).

37. *Allognathosuchus* image adapted from http://idata.over-blog.com/0/53/79/85/sij72-6c.gif; *Telmatornis* image adapted from "Telmatornis priscus" by Scott Reid (2018) via drawingwithdinosaurs.tumblr.com.

38. *Hyposaurus* image adapted from "Tethyan Seacroc (Hyposaurus sp.) by Russell J. Hawley via www.paleonature.org; *Mosasaurus* image adapted from https://dinosaurpictures.org/mosasaurus-pictures; *Elasmosaurus* image adapted from figure 8 in Sachs and Kear (2015); *Tylosaurus* image adapted from "Tylosalurus-proriger.jpg" by DiBgd (2015) via Wikimedia Commons licensed under CC BY-SA 4.0.

39. Image adapted from Muratart/istockphoto posted at https://www.sciencenews.org/sites/default/files/2018/05/main/articles/052418_LH_chixculub_feat.jpg.

TABLE 1

VERTEBRATE FOSSILS DESCRIBED FROM THE MESOZOIC STRATA OF VIRGINIA AND NEARBY STATES

LOWER CARNIAN (16 taxa)

FISH

Cionichthys meekeri (Va.)

Dictyopyge macrura (Va.)

cf. *Diplurus* sp. (Va.)

Lissodus sp. (Va.)

Tanaocrossus sp. (Va.)

AMPHIBIANS

Calamops paludosus (Pa.)

PROCOLOPHONIDS

Gomphiosauridion baileyae (Va.)

Xenodiphiodon petraios (Va.)

LACERTILIANS

Lepidosauria indet. (Va.)

ARCHOSAURS

Doswellia kaltenbachi (Va.)

Euscolosuchus olseni (Va.)

Phytosauridae (probably *Angistorhinus* or *Parasuchus*) (Va.)

Poposaurus gracilis (Va.)

Uatchitodon kroeleri (Va.)

Table 1: Vertebrate fossils described from the Mesozoic strata of Virginia and nearby states.

THERAPSIDS

Boreogomphodon jeffersoni (Va.)

Microconodon tenuirostris (Va.)

UPPER CARNIAN (31 taxa)

FISH

Arganodus sp. (N.C.)

Cionichthys sp. (N.C., Va.)

Diplurus longicaudatus (Va.)

Diplurus newarki (N.C.)

Pariostegus sp. (N.C.)

Semionotus sp. (N.C., Va.)

Synorichthys sp. (N.C., Va.)

Turseodus sp. (N.C., Va.)

AMPHIBIANS

Dictyocephalus elegans (N.C.)

PROCOLOPHONIDS

Colognathus obscurus (N.C.)

LACERTILIANS

Sphenodontidae indet. (Va.)

PRIMITIVE AND/OR POORLY KNOWN
ARCHOSAUROMORPHS

Crosbysaurus sp. (N.C.)

Galtonia gibbidens (N.C.)

Mecistotrachelos apeoros (Va.)

Revueltosaurus olseni (N.C.)

Tanytrachelos ahynis (= *Gwynnedosaurus erici?*) (N.C., Va.)

Uatchitodon schneideri (N.C.)

RAUISUCHIDS
Postosuchus allisonae (N.C.)

Zatomus sarcophagus (N.C.)

AETOSAURS
Coahomasuchus sp. (N.C.)

Gorgetosuchus pekinensis (N.C.)

Lucasuchus sp. (N.C.)

PHYTOSAURS
Rutiodon carolinensis (N.C., Va.)

CROCODYLOMORPHA
Carnufex carolinensis (N.C.)

Dromicosuchus grallator (N.C.)

THEROPODS
Banisterobates boisseaui (footprints) (Va.)

Atreipus cf. *A. milfordensis* (footprints) (Va.)

Grallator isp. (footprints) (Va.)

THERAPSIDS
aff. *Placerias* sp. (N.C.)

Boreogomphodon jeffersoni (=*Plinthogomphodon herpetairus*) (N.C.)

Microconodon tenuirostris (N.C.)

NORIAN (18 taxa)

FISHES
Cionichthys sp. (Va.)

Tanaocrossus sp. (Va.)

Semionotus sp. (Va.)

Diplurus newarki (Va.)

LACERTILIANS
Rhynchosauroides brunswickii (footprints) (Va.)

TANYSTROPHEIDS

Gwyneddichnium majore (likely *Gwyneddosaurus/ Tanytrachelos* footprints) (Va.)

RAUISUCHIDS

Chirotherium lulli (footprints) (Va.)

AETOSAURS

Aetosaurus arcuatus (dermal armor scale) (Va.)

Brachychirotherium parvum (footprints) (Va.)

PHYTOSAURS

Apatopus lineatus (fossils and footprints) (Va.)

DINOSAURS

THEROPODS

Grallator sillimani (footprints) (Va.)

Grallator tenuis (footprints) (Va.)

Grallator tuberosus (footprints) (Va.)

Kayentapus minor (footprints) (Va.)

Plesiornis pilulatus (footprints) (Va.)

PROSAUROPODS

Plateosauridae (gastroliths) (Va.)

ORNITHISCHIANS

Anomoepus aff. *A. isodactylus* (footprints) (Va.)

THERAPSIDS

Pentasauropus isp. (footprints) (Pa.)

HETTANGIAN (13 taxa)

FISHES

Ptycholepis marshi (Va.)

Redfieldius gracilis (Va.)

Semionotus elegans (Va.)

Semionotus micropterus (Va.)

Semionotus tenuiceps (Va.)

Diplurus longicaudatus (Va.)

CROCODYLOMORPHA

Batrachopus deweyi (footprints) (Va.)

DINOSAURS

THEROPODS

Grallator parallelus (footprints) (Va.)

Grallator sillimani (footprints) (Va.)

Grallator tuberosus (footprints) (Va.)

Kayentapus minor (footprints) (Va.)

PROSAUROPODS

Eubrontes giganteus (footprints) (Va.)

ORNITHISCHIANS

Anomoepus scambus (footprints) (Va.)

ALBIAN (31 taxa)

SHARKS

Egertonodus basanus (Md.)

Hybodus ensis (Md.)

BONY FISHES

Ceratodus kranzi (Md.)

Lepidotes sp. (Md.)

aff. *Paraelops cearensis* (Va.)

Vidalamiinae indet. (Md.)

AMPHIBIANS

Anura indet. (footprints) (Va.)

Table 1: Vertebrate fossils described from the Mesozoic strata of Virginia and nearby states.

TURTLES

Arundelemys dardeni (Md.)

Emydhippus isp. (likely these are footprints
of *Arundelemys* or *Glyptops*) (Va.)

Glyptops caelatus (Md.)

Naomichelys sp. (Md.)

CROCODILES

Bernissartiidae indet. (Md.)

Goniopholidae indet. (Md.)

Pholidosauridae indet. (Md.)

PTEROSAURIA

Pteraichnus isp. (footprints) (Md.)

DINOSAURS

THEROPODS

Acrocanthosaurus sp. (Md.)

Deinonychus sp. (Md.)

Gypsichnites pacensis (footprints) (Va.)

Ornithomimosauria morphotype A (Md.)

Ornithomimosauria morphotype B (Md.)

Ornithomimipus angustus (large ornithomimosaurian
footprint) (Va.)

Ornithomimipus jaillardi (small ornithomimosaurian
footprint) (Va.)

Irenesauripus glenrosensis (likely tracks of *Acrocanthosaurus*) (Va.)

Tyrannosauripus bachmani (footprints) (Va.)

Richardoestesia sp. (Md.)

SAUROPODS

Astrodon johnstoni (Md.)

Brontopodus birdi (footprints of *Astrodon*) (Va.)

ANKYLOSAURS

Proplanoprosaurus marylandicus (Md.)

Priconodon crassus (Md.)

Tetrasauropodus borealis (ankylosaur footprints) (Va.)

ORNITHOPODS

Caririchnium kortmeyeri (footprints) (Va.)

Hadrosauropodus leonardi (footprints) (Va.)

Hypsiloichnus marylandica (footprints) (Md., Va.)

Tenontosaurus sp. (Md.). (likely maker of *Caririchnium kortmeyeri* footprints)

CERATOPSIANS

Neoceratopsia indet. (Md.)

MAMMALS

Arundelconodon hottoni (Md.)

Argillomys marylandensis (Md.)

CENOMANIAN (7 taxa)

PTEROSAURS

Pteraichnus isp. (footprints) (Md.)

DINOSAURS

THEROPODS

Irenesauripus isp. (footprints) (N.J.)

ANKYLOSAURS

Tetrapodosaurus isp. (footprints) (Md.)

BIRDS

Aquatilavipes isp. (footprints) (Md.)

MAMMALS

Sederipes goddardensis (footprints) (Md.)

Morphotype B (footprints) (Md.)

Morphotype C (footprints) (Md.)

CAMPANIAN (105 taxa)

SHARKS

Asteracanthus sp. (N.C.)

Carcharias holmdelensis (Del.)

Carcharias samhammeri (Del., N.C., N.J.)

Cretodus arcuata (N.J.)

Cretodus borodini (Del., N.J.)

Cretolamna appendiculata (N.J., N.C.)

Cretodus arcuatus (Md.)

Cretodus borodini (Md.)

Galeorhinus sp. (N.C.)

Ginglymostoma globidens (Del., N.C.)

Hybodus montanensis (N.C.)

Hybodus sp. (Del., N.C., N.J.)

Lissodus babulskii (Del., N.J.)

Lonchidion sp. (Del., N.C., N.J.)

Odontaspis aculeatus (Del., N.C.)

Paranomotodon angustidens (Del., N.J.)

Proplatyrhina sp. (N.C.)

Pseudocorax granti (Del., N.J.)

Rhinobatos casieri (Del., N.C.)

Scapanorhyncus texanus (Del., N.J., N.C.)

Squalicorax kaupi (Del., N.J., N.C., S.C.)

Squalicorax pristodontus (Del., N.C., S.C.)

Squatina hassei (Del., N.C., N.J., S.C.)

Synodontaspis holmdelensis (N.J., N.C.)

RAYS

Borodinopristis schwimmeri (N.J., N.C., S.C.)

Brachyrhizodus witchitaensis (Del., N.J., N.C., S.C.)

Dasyatis sp. (N.C.)

Ischyodus bifurcatus (Del., N.J., N.C.)

Ischyrhiza avonicola (Del., N.C., S.C.)

Ischyrhiza mira (Del., N.J., N.C., S.C.)

Protoplatyrhina sp. (N.J.)

Pseudohypolophus sp. (Del., N.J.)

Ptychotrygon hooveri (N.J.)

Ptychotrygon triangulata (N.C.)

Ptychotrygon vermiculata (Del., N.J.)

Rhombodus binkhorsti (N.C.)

Rhombodus levis (Del., N.J., N.C.)

Sclerorhynchus sp. (Del., N.J., N.C.)

Schizorhiza sp. (N.C.)

BONY FISHES

Acipenser sp. (N.J., N.C.)

Albula sp. (N.J., N.C.)

Amia cf. *A. fragosa* (N.J.)

Anomoeodus phaseolus (N.J., Del., N.C., S.C.)

Atractosteus occidentalis (N.J.)

cf. *Cimolichthyes* sp. (N.J.)

Cylindracanthus ornatus (N.C.)

Enchodus ferox (Del., N.C.)

Enchodus petrosus (N.J., N.C., S.C.)

Hadrodus priscus (N.J., Del., N.C., S.C.)

Lepisosteus sp. (Del., N.C.)

Megacoelacanthus dobei (N.J.)

Paralbula casei (N.J., Del., N.C., S.C.)

cf. *Platacodon* sp. (N.J.)

Saurodon sp. (N.C.)

Xiphactinus vetus (N.J., N.C.)

FROGS

Hylidae indet. (N.J.)

cf. *Eopelobates* sp. (N.J.)

cf. *Discoglossus* sp. (N.J.)

TURTLES

Adocus beatus (N.J., N.C.)

Atlantochelys mortoni (N.J.)

Bothremys barberi (N.J., N.C.)

Chedighaii sp. (N.C.)

Chedighaii barberi (N.J.)

Corsochelys bentleyi (N.J., S.C.)

Euclastes wielandi (N.J.)

Taphrosphys dares (N.C.)

"*Trionyx*" *halophilus* (N.J., Md., N.C.)

"*Trionyx*" *priscus* (N.J., S.C.)

PLESIOSAURS

Elasmosauridae indet. (N.C.)

LIZARDS

Prototeius stageri (N.J.)

cf. *Haptosphenus* sp. (N.J.)

Iguanidae indet. (N.J.)

Xenosauridae indet. (N.J.)

Helodermatidae indet. (N.J.)

Anguinae indet. (N.J.)

Necrosauridae indet. (N.J.)

MOSASAURS

Clidastes sp. (Del.)

Globidens sp. (Del.)

Halisaurus sp. (N.C.)

Platecarpus sp. (N.C.)

Prognathodon sp. (N.C.)

Tylosaurus sp. (Del., N.C.)

SNAKES

Coniophis sp. (N.C.)

CROCODILIANS

Borealosuchus threensis (Del., N.J., N.C.)

Brachychampsa sp. (N.J., N.C.)

Deinosuchus rugosus (N.J., N.C.)

Thoracosaurus neocessariensis (N.J., N.C.)

PTEROSAURS

aff. *Pteranodon* sp. (Del.)

Arambourgiania philadelphiae (Tenn.)

DINOSAURS

THEROPODS

Appalachiosaurus montgomeriensis (N.C., S.C.)

Dryptosaurus aquilunguis (N.J., N.C.)

Ornithomimus sp. (N.J., N.C.)

Saurornitholestes langstoni (N.C., S.C.)

ORNITHOPODS

Lophorhothon sp. (N.C.)

Hadrosaurus foulkii (N.J., N.C.)

"Hadrosaurus" minor (N.C.)

Hypsibema crassicauda (N.J., N.C.)

ANKYLOSAURS

Nodosauridae indet. (N.J.)

CERATOPSIANS

Leptoceratopsidae indet. (N.C.)

MAMMALS

MULTITUBERCULATA

cf. *Cimolodon* sp. (N.J.)

Cimolomyidae indet. (N.J.)

Cimolomys sp. (N.C.)

cf. *Mesodma* sp. (N.J.)

METATHERIA

Stagodontidae indet. (N.J.)

EUTHERIA

Eutheria indet. (N.J.)

MAASTRICHTIAN (112 taxa)

SHARKS

Anomotodon cf. *A. toddi* (N.C.)

Cantioscyllium decipiens (Md.)

Cantioscyllium cf. *C. meyeri* (N.C.)

Carcharias samhammeri (Md., N.C.)

Carcharias holmdelensis (Md.)

Chiloscyllium greeni (Md.)

Cretolamna appendiculata (N.J., Del., Md., N.C.)

Cretolamna biauriculata (Md.)

Cretolamna marroccana (N.C.)

Cretodus arcuatus (Md., N.C.)

Cretodus borodini (Md.)

Ewingia problematica (Md.)

Galeorhinus girardoti (Md.)

Ginglymostoma globidens (Md.)

Ginglymostoma lehneri (Md.)

Heterodontus granti (Md., N.C.)

Hybodus sp. (N.J., Md., N.C.)

Hypotodus sp. (Md.)

Notidanodon sp. (N.C.)

Odontaspis aculeatus (Md., N.C.)

Palaeogaleus sp. (N.C.)

Plicatoscyllium antiquum (Md., N.C.)

Plicatoscyllium derameei (Md., N.C.)

Pseudocorax granti (Del.)

Pseudocorax cf. *P. affinis* (N.C.)

Pseudohypolophus mcnultyi (Md.)

Scapanorhyncus texanus (N.J., Md., N.C.)

Serratolamna serrata (Md., N.C.)

Squalicorax kaupi (N.J., Md., N.C.)

Squalicorax pristodontus (N.J., Md., N.C.)

Squalus huntensis (N.C.)

Squatina hassei (Md.)

RAYS

Dasyatis commercensis (Md., N.C.)

Ischyodus bifurcatus (Md.)

Ischyrhiza avonicola (Md., N.C.)

Ischyrhiza mira (Md., N.C.)

Myliobatis sp. (Md.)

Ptycotrygon clementsi (N.C.)

Ptycotrygon vermiculata (Md.)

Raja farishi (Md., N.C.)

Rhinobatos sp. (Md., N.C.)

Rhombodus binkhorsti (Md., N.C.)

Sclerorhynchus cf. *S. pettersi* (N.C.)

BONY FISHES

Albula sp. (N.J., Md.)

Ampheristis (Md.)

Anguilla? (Md.)

Anomoeodus phaseolus (N.J., Md.)

Apateodus (Md.)

Argyroberyx? (Md.)

Arius? (Md.)

Ceratodus aff. *C. frazieri* (N.J.)

Congrophichthus (Md.)

Cowetaichthys (Md.)

Cylindracanthus ornatus (Md.)

Enchodus ferox (Md., N.C.)

Eutawichthys (Md.)

Hadrodus priscus (N.J., Md.)

Holocentronotus (Md.)

Hoplopteryx (Md.)

Hoplostethus (Md.)

Ichthyotringa? (Md.)

Kokenichthys (Md.)

Lepisosteus sp. (Md.)

Muraenanguilla (Md.)

Osmeroides (Md.)

Ossulcus (Md.)

Otolithopsis (Md.)

Palaeogadus (Md.)

Paralbula casei (N.J., Md.)

Paraulopus (Md.)

Pempheris? (Md.)

*Pterothrissus (*Md.)

Severnichthys (Md.)

Vorhisia sp. (Md.)

TURTLES

Adocus beatus (N.J.)

Agomphus pectoralis (N.J.)

Bothremys cooki (N.J.)

Corsochelys sp. (N.J.)

Euclastes wielandi (N.J., Md.)

Osteopygis emarginatus (N.J., Md.)

Neptunochelys tuberosus (N.J.)

Peritresius ornatus (N.J., Md.)

Pneumatoarthrus peloreus (N.J.)

Prionochelys nauta (N.J.)

Taphrosphys sulcatus (N.J.)

"Trionyx" halophilus (N.J., Md.)

"Trionyx" priscus (Md.)

PLESIOSAURS

Cimoliasaurus magnus (N.J., Md., N.C.)

MOSASAURS

Halisaurus platyspondylus (N.J., Md.)

Liodon sectorius (N.J.)

Mosasaurus conodon (N.J.)

Mosasaurus dekayi (N.J., Md.)

Mosasaurus hoffmanni (= *M. maximus*) (N.J., Md.)

Platycarpus sp. (N.J.)

Plioplatecarpus marshi (= *P. depressus*) (N.J.)

Prognathodon rapax (N.J., Md.)

CROCODILIANS

Allognathosuchus sp. (Md.)

Bottosaurus harlani (Md.)

Deinosuchus rugosus (Md.)

Hyposaurus rogersii (N.J., Md.)

Thoracosaurus neocessariensis (N.J., Md.)

PTEROSAURS

Arambourgiania philadelphiae (N.J.)

Azhdarcho sp. (N.C.)

DINOSAURS
  THEROPODS
    Dryptosaurus aquilunguis (N.J., N.C.)
    "Ornithomimus" antiquus (Md., N.C.)

  ORNITHOPODS
    Hadrosaurus foulki (Md., N.J.)
    "Hadrosaurus" minor (N.J.)
    Lambeosaurinae indet. (N.J.)

  ANKYLOSAURS
    Nodosauridae indet. (N.J.)

  CERATOPSIANS
    Ceratopsidae indet. (Miss.)

BIRDS
  Telmatornis priscus (N.J.)

MAMMALS
  MULTITUBERCULATA
    Multituberculate femur indet. (N.J.)

ABOUT THE AUTHOR

Robert E. Weems grew up in Ashland, Virginia. In the second grade, he read a book called *All About Dinosaurs* by Roy Chapman Andrews and from then on became determined to learn all he could about dinosaurs in Virginia and nearby states. He received a bachelor's degree in biology from Randolph-Macon College in 1968, a master's degree in geology from Virginia Tech in 1972, and a doctoral degree in geology from the George Washington University in 1978. Dr. Weems worked for the U.S. Geological Survey in Reston, Virginia, from 1978 until 2010, studying and mapping the stratigraphy of piedmont and coastal plain strata in the eastern United States. Since then, he has spent much of his retirement continuing research on the age of dinosaurs in and around Virginia.